Naturally
Fun Parties
for kids

Published by Sellers Publishing, Inc.

Text and photos © 2012 Anni Daulter
All rights reserved.

Photo styling by Anni Daulter

Sellers Publishing, Inc.
161 John Roberts Road, South Portland, Maine 04106
Visit our Web site: www.sellerspublishing.com • E-mail: rsp@rsvp.com

ISBN: 13: 978-1-4162-0656-9
e-ISBN: 978-1-4162-0737-5
Library of Congress Control Number: 2011935639

10 9 8 7 6 5 4 3 2 1

Printed and bound in China.

Naturally
Fun Parties
for kids

Creating Handmade, Earth-Friendly
Celebrations for All Seasons
and Occasions

Anni Daulter
with Heather Fontenot

Photography by
Tnah & Mario Di Donato

SELLERS
PUBLISHING

Contents

Spring Parties

Summer Parties

Autumn Parties

Winter Parties

Welcome

Welcome to *Naturally Fun Parties for Kids*, a book that we hope will provide parents with a lot of unique ideas for celebrating with their families throughout the year. The parties are inspired by nature, are cost-effective, practice sustainable efforts such as recycling and upcycling, and are downright adorable! We are excited to share these pages with you and hope that they inspire you to think outside the traditional party box for your next celebration. Have fun with these ideas, reinterpret them to fit your families, and most of all, remember that keeping it simple will allow more space and time for the celebrations to be truly enjoyed and appreciated by all.

This book uses nature as the backdrop for most of its celebrations and the parties are organized into seasons. We offer tips and tricks for making the parties green, natural, simple, and organic in style and content. Although there are some party themes here that are specifically geared toward girls or boys, they do not need to be gender-specific and can be easily adapted to include all children. Since most of the children we know do not like to sit quietly at a beautifully decorated table, most of the parties reflect a more simple approach that allows for a food table or space that children can grab and go from, but you can still make that look fun and seasonal! As you create your own celebrations, feel free to mix and match the various party elements to produce your own perfect party.

Now go have fun!

Anni and Heather

Party Tips to Get You Started

Thrift stores: other folks leftovers can be your found treasures

I love going thrifting. I like to look for old cashmere sweaters that can be upcycled into a million things (pillows, dolls, purses, aprons), silk shirts that can be torn into strips for party banners, old canning jars, dishes, cutting boards, baskets, and other goodies that pop up in thrift stores. You'll be surprised at how handy these items are when pulling together a wide variety of parties.

Save glass jars and tin cans

Save all sizes and shapes for use in numerous ways! Take the labels off and thoroughly clean these recycled gems and store them in a container for a later date. When it's time to create a party, you have immediate access to unique bottles that can be used both for table decorations or hanging vases, and tin cans that can be lined with parchment paper and used as a simple container for sweet potato fries or as a holder for other small elements.

Save your old dresses, shirts, and scarves for repurposing

I have a huge bin filled with clothes that can be cut up and repurposed for any use. My kids have access to it to play and create, and I dive in whenever I want to make a party banner, upcycle a sweater sleeve into a small pouch, or try a new craft idea. Just because it may not fit your fashion style anymore, doesn't mean it won't make the perfect bag, banner, or apron!

Borrow

If you were planning a party and lived near me, I would say stop by and go "shopping." I love sharing and I borrow from my friends all the time. You would be surprised what your friends may have and might let you borrow. When I was creating this book, I called my friend Rose to ask if I could borrow a couple of tablecloths for the Summer Solstice Beach Party. She invited me over and showed me to her shed. She had about twenty boxes, color-coded, of just tablecloths! Her son Wes was very happy I was borrowing a few and told me not to bring them back, as he thought his mother had a serious issue with overbuying tablecloths. So ask your friends and family if they happen to have that certain something you need for a party — you'll be surprised what is available for borrowing.

Keep a collection of nature items on hand

When my children and I go on hikes and walks, we always collect nature goodies like sticks, pods, fallen acorns or pinecones, shells from the beach, special rocks, and any other nature goodies we can find. For my daughter's birthday one year, I made all the guests their own fairy houses just from found sticks, fallen bark from trees, and other nature treasures. They were fabulous and did not cost me anything to make!

Use nature as the backdrop of your celebrations

Let Mother Nature decorate for you! When you set up your parties in your garden, at the beach, a creek, a riverbank, a farm, a forest, your backyard, or even nestled in front of a fireplace, you have the ready-made setting for a beautiful party. The wonders of nature create a landscape that everyone appreciates and a natural playground for kids to explore.

A note about invites

I like old-fashioned, hand-delivered invitations, where each one is crafted with love and care and is a sneak-peek into the celebration to come. When I got married, I hand-painted every invitation on mini canvases (and put it together like a little journal of our lives together). People loved these invites so much, many of them kept them out for others to see as an artpiece. I also love the idea of three-dimensional invitations, which you'll see examples of in some of the parties in this book.

A note about food

Coming up with seasonal fare is always best at parties because it ensures you are getting the freshest produce with the ripest flavors. It's also often the healthiest choice. I like to try to buy from my local farmers' markets, CSA's, and co-ops and keep the food organic, tasty, fresh, and simple. Making party food also gives you some opportunities to get creative and have fun, like using mini pumpkins as the soup bowl at a autumn-inspired celebration.

Budding Spring

Welcome to Spring! The budding of this colorful season brings new life with the sun shining, flowers blooming, kids climbing trees and skinning their knees, and new seedlings being planted in the garden. The spring equinox, on or near March 21, is a day of equal day and night, a day on which the sun and the earth are in balance with one another. This is a great time to gather together to mark the changing of the seasons and welcome the light after a dark and cold winter. It's a time of renewal and rebirth. Some symbols that mark these changes are seeds, eggs, and new life. Using nature as the backdrop for your spring celebrations means gorgeous rose and lavender gardens, forests, parks, and even the comfort of your own backyard. So take off your winter coat and warm up to all of the sunny opportunities spring has to offer.

The beauty of Spring is…

forest faeries fluttering about the riverbanks; worms crawling around the **freshly tilled garden**; girls giggling while whispering secrets and picking **wildflowers**; boys making mud pies and digging in the earth just for the pure joy of **getting dirty**; the sun peeking through the clouds with the promise of endless hours of play…

Egg-Dyeing Spring Garden Party

You're Invited . . .

to spend the afternoon in the rose garden, coloring and hiding eggs, snacking on mini quiches and potted breads and jam, and enjoying refreshing lemon ice pops! Whether you celebrate Easter or just the coming of spring, coloring and hiding eggs is a traditional celebration that can pull together friends and reawaken your creative spirit.

The Inspiration

As the sun begins to peek over the winter hills, melting snow and offering promises of playtime outside, it's a great time to gather children together to mark this seasonal excitement. Springtime is like a breath of fresh air and a renewed sense of budding life, and kids will love marking this time with a day of natural egg dyeing.

PROJECTS AND MATERIALS

Egg-shaped invitations in cozy pocket pouches
- old or recycled sweaters
- needle and thread
- watercolor paper and watercolors
- stamp of word "egg" (or letter stamps) and ink pad
- press-on letters or markers
- ribbon or floral embellishments

Spring fabric banner
- recycled clothing or scrap fabric in spring colors and patterns
- rope or yarn

Inspirational sign
- repurposed fabric (single light color works best)
- natural sticks
- hot glue and hot glue gun

Table decor
- recycled glass bottles
- recycled clothing or scrap fabric
- fresh spring flowers

Egg-dyeing activity
- eggs
- fruits, vegetables, and spices to make egg dye (Note: Homemade dyes take time to come to full saturation, so prepare the dyes the day before your party.)
- canning jars

Recipes
- Flowerpot Cheese Breads (baked in mini terra-cotta pots)
- Egg-tastic! Mushroom and Onion Mini Crustless Quiches
- Garden Cooler Lemon-Mint Ice Pops

TIMELINE

2 weeks prior to event:
- choose your location
- create invites and hand them out

1 week prior to event:
- gather table decor and dishware
- make fabric banner
- make inspirational sign

Day prior to event:
- make all dyes
- boil eggs (to be dyed)
- make ice pops

Day of event:
- set up egg-dyeing station and food table
- hang banner and signs
- make potted breads
- prepare quiches, but cook them 40 minutes prior to serving

Create Invitations

- Have your child paint a large piece of watercolor paper with watercolors in spring shades. When the paper is dry, cut egg-shaped cards from the paper.

- Stamp the word "egg" on each piece of paper, and use press-on letters to write the word "party." Handwrite the date and time of your party and address on the back of each egg card.

- Cut the end of a sleeve off of an old sweater, sew one side closed with an easy topstitch, and leave one side open to make a pocket large enough to slide your invitation into. Make one of these pockets to use as an envelope for each invitation.

- Add embellishments (such as a small felt flower or a button) to the pocket and decorative topstitching to the invitation, if desired.

- If you'd like, tie the whole pocket with a ribbon so it looks like a little package and the invite doesn't fall out.

Set the Scene

If you host your spring party in a garden, you won't need much more for decor, as nature has provided it for you. A **rose or lavender garden** works beautifully. If you do not have access to a flower garden, consider hosting it in your backyard with **fresh cut spring flowers** from your local farmers' market.

If you have a natural wood table to set up in the garden, consider leaving it as is. If you want to use a tablecloth, you may be able to pick one up at a thrift store. A **simple and recycled tablecloth** is best since you will soon have canning jars full of gorgeous egg dyes to add to the setting.

Make a fabric banner: Tear strips of slightly uneven lengths and widths (think wide ribbons) of old shirts or dresses or scrap fabric that has a springlike pattern. Tie strips along a rope and hang the rope up from tree to tree to create a lovely spring banner to float on the breeze.

Repurpose a piece of fabric and gather some sticks or twigs to create a fun **seasonal or inspirational sign** showcasing a single word such as "joy." Use a hot glue gun to affix the sticks to the fabric.

Tie fabric strips (extras from those you used to create your banner) around recycled glass bottles. Fill **fabric-wrapped bottles with fresh cut spring flowers** and place on the food table.

Make Natural Dyes to Dye Eggs

You can create beautifully colored eggs from what you may already have in your kitchen and garden. It's fun for children (and adults) to see all the rich colors that naturally come from fruits, vegetables, and spices. All you need is a little vinegar, some pots, a strainer, and lots of jars.

You may wish to ask each child attending the party to bring a basket of eggs to dye, which will provide plenty of eggs to color, hide, and find. However, if the eggs don't arrive until the beginning of the party, you will have to hard-boil them during the party, which may take away time from the rest of the activities.

Make the dye:

Fruits and vegetables need time to simmer to extract their natural colors; some need to simmer for several hours to reach full color potential. For each fruit or vegetable below, you will follow the same simple procedure: Combine the required amount of dye source material, 1–2 quarts water, and ¼ cup white vinegar. Combine the materials in a large pot, bring to a boil, reduce heat, and simmer for several hours until desired color is reached. Strain dye into a canning jar to cool. Here are the specific formulas for some beautiful dyes:

Red Onion Skins for deep rose dye:
5 cups red onion skins + 2 quarts water +
   ¼ cup white vinegar

Red Cabbage for deep blue dye:
1 red cabbage head chopped + 2 quarts water +
   ¼ cup white vinegar

Fresh Beets for pink dye:
5 beets, chopped + 2 quarts water +
   ¼ cup white vinegar

Frozen Blueberries for violet dye:
5 cups blueberries, frozen and left whole +
   1 quart water + ¼ cup white vinegar

Turmeric (spice) for yellow dye:
4 tablespoons turmeric + 1 quart water +
   ¼ cup white vinegar

Coffee for golden brown dye:
4 tablespoons ground coffee +
   1 quart water + ¼ cup white vinegar

Paprika (spice) for orange dye:
4 tablespoons paprika + 1 quart water +
   ¼ cup white vinegar

Cool Combos:
Blueberry dye mixed with turmeric dye gives you
   an olive green egg.

Red cabbage dye mixed with turmeric dye gives
   you a very deep green egg.

Hard-boil the eggs:
Place eggs in a big pot of cold water and set over medium-high heat. Once the water reaches a rolling boil, leave the eggs in the boiling water for another 10 minutes. Remove eggs from water and set aside to cool and dry.

Decorate the eggs:
Set jars of dye in the middle of a table. Dip the eggs into various colors. The longer the eggs remain in the dye, the darker the colors will become. For very deep colors, soak eggs in dye overnight. Set colored eggs aside to dry completely before the egg hunt festivities begin.

Food Fun and Recipes

Baking the cheese breads in mini terra-cotta flowerpots (about $1.00 each) reinforces the spring garden theme, plus it's a fun way to serve individual bread portions. Using eggs as the base for one of the party's recipes keeps the theme going, so make mini quiches. Offering a refreshing Lemon-Mint Ice Pop is a great way to give a sweet treat to finish up a warm afternoon of work and play!

FLOWERPOT CHEESE BREADS

I bake these in small terra-cotta pots that are 7 inches tall with a 5-inch opening across the top.

3½ cups warm water

2 teaspoons yeast

½ cup mozzarella cheese

⅓ cup ricotta cheese

⅓ cup feta cheese

handful of fresh thyme

4 cups bread flour

2½ teaspoons salt

2 tablespoons melted butter

1 teaspoon honey

olive oil to rub the inside
  of the bowl and pots

6 small terra-cotta pots

fresh whole herbs for decoration

In a large bowl, combine the warm water and yeast and let sit for 5 minutes.

While yeast is sitting, mix together all three cheeses and thyme in a separate bowl and set aside.

To the bowl with the yeast, stir in 2 cups of the flour, salt, and butter. Add the remaining 2 cups flour and honey, and mix into a dough. On a lightly floured surface, knead the dough for about 10 minutes.

Coat a large, clean bowl with olive oil, place dough inside, and cover with a damp towel. Let sit until it has doubled in size, about 1 hour.

Preheat oven to 450°F.

Remove the dough from the bowl, press out the excess gas from the dough, and knead for another 5 minutes. Cut the dough into 6 equal pieces, each the size needed to fill about half a small terra-cotta pot. Test dough pieces for size, but don't yet put them into pots.

Roll out the dough pieces to approximately 6–8 inches across and ¼ inch thick, and place cheese and herb mixture in the center of each. Fold each side in toward the middle in order to enclose the cheese mixture in the dough. Press together the seams with a little water to make a small package.

Coat each pot with a little olive oil, then line the bottom and sides with parchment paper. Place each filled dough ball in a pot, put pots on a cookie sheet, and drizzle dough tops with olive oil. Squirt each bread ball with water from a spray bottle, and lay herbs on top.

Bake for 25 minutes or until golden brown. Serve with your favorite jam.

Makes 6 breads

Egg-tastic! Mushroom and Onion Mini Crustless Quiches

I use small ramekins (5 inches in diameter, 1 inch tall, 4-ounce capacity) for this recipe, but you can use a jumbo muffin pan as well.

1 tablespoon unsalted butter, plus extra for coating ramekins

1 cup chopped yellow onion

3 garlic cloves, minced

2 cups chopped fresh mushrooms (any variety you like)

¼ teaspoon ground pepper

2 pinches sea salt

2 tablespoons Bragg Liquid Aminos

6 eggs

¼ cup milk

¾ cup freshly grated Parmesan cheese

Preheat oven to 350°F. Lightly butter bottom and sides of 6 ramekins.

In a large saucepan, melt butter over medium heat and immediately add the onions to start browning. After a few minutes, add garlic and stir until lightly browned.

Add mushrooms, pepper, salt, and Bragg's. Cook for approximately 4 minutes to brown mushrooms. Set aside.

In a large mixing bowl, mix together eggs, milk, and cheese. Add the mushroom mixture and stir to combine. Ladle egg mixture into individual ramekins and bake for 35–40 minutes or until browned on top.

Serves 6

Garden Cooler Lemon-Mint Ice Pops

**4 cups fresh lemonade (juice of 8 lemons,
preferabley Meyers, mixed with 1 quart
water and 4 tablespoons raw agave nectar)**

¼ cup fresh mint leaves

¼ cup grated lemon zest

Pour lemonade into blender, add mint, and blend together. Pour mixture into chosen (4-ounce) pop molds and add lemon zest for texture. Add sticks to pops and freeze. (If using paper cups, you'll need to let the mixture freeze halfway before adding the stick.)

Makes 8 (4-ounce) pops

pancakes

are...

delicious

Fluffy

gooey

sticky + **FUN**

Pancake P.J. Party

You're Invited . . .

to meet in your pajamas; decorate stacks of pancakes with fun, yummy toppings; gobble up healthy donuts (yes, there is such a thing!); and hop around doing silly sack races!

The Inspiration

A good friend's daughter wanted to have a sleepover party, but my friend thought she was too young. I suggested the kids come to a morning party dressed in P.J.'s (as if they had spent the night), have pancakes and other morning treats, and enjoy a high-energy morning gathering, without the sleep deprivation that often comes with a full sleepover party.

PROJECTS AND MATERIALS

Printed paper invitations
- printable pieces of scrapbooking paper (available at art supply stores)
- computer with word processing program and color printer
- hole punch
- satin ribbon

Outside decor
- cupcake holders that match your color theme
- satin ribbon
- scissors
- ice bucket to hold various milks and ice

Table decor
- sunflowers
- white plates
- various small baskets and bowls for toppings
- classic checkered tablecloth

Games
- flour or potato sacks, oversized pillowcases, or child-size sleeping bags for sack races

Recipes
- Whole Wheat Sour Cream Pancakes with Blackberry Agave Syrup (and multiple toppings)
- Chocolate Donuts with Lemon Glaze and Vanilla Cake Donuts with Strawberry Goop
- Mini Artichoke Dips with Rustic Bread

TIMELINE

2 weeks prior to event:
- choose your location
- create invites and hand them out

1 week prior to event:
- gather table decor and dishware
- make hanging cupcake wrapper decorations
- make labels for pancake toppings to let guests know all the possibilities
- gather sacks for races

Day prior to event:
- make sunflower arrangements for the tables
- make donuts
- prep artichoke dip (but don't bake)
- gather all pancake toppings
- make blackberry agave syrup

Day of event:
- hang cupcake string decorations
- set up food table
- make pancakes
- bake artichoke dip
- set up toppings

Create Invitations

- Using your computer's word porcessing program, find a fun font and color to create a simple text document that gives the details of your party. Include an image that matches your theme, if you like. I used a picture of a stack of pancakes that I took. (If it's not your artwork, make sure you get permission to use it.)

- Print out the invitations on pieces of decorative scrapbooking paper, using a color printer and punch two holes in the top corners of each invitation. Thread a satin ribbon through the holes, make a large loop, and tie off at the top so guests can hang the invite if desired.

- Hand-deliver these special invitations to all the friends invited!

Set the Scene

A Pancake P.J. party can take place anywhere. You can host it **indoors or outdoors** depending on the weather and the size of your guest list. The most important element for this party is a huge stack of pancakes and lots of toppings. I liked making this party a bit retro, hosting it with the use of my friend's funky camper parked at a park. I chose a yellow and turquoise color palette to accent the day.

Make **homemade party streamers** using cupcake papers in your chosen color theme and some pretty satin ribbon. Turn the cupcake paper upside down, poke a hole in the middle of the base, and string it with a piece of ribbon. Tie knots on the inside of the cupcake holder after threading each one to hold it in place on the ribbon. Each string should have several cupcake holders. Make several streamers.

Use **spring flowers**, such as daffodils or tulips, and **herbs** to decorate the tables.

Use **checkered tablecloths** and **real white plates** so the kids can easily see their pancake creations. You can often find inexpensive plates at thrift stores and then save them for future use at parties.

Find a spot, such as a low branch, to hang the collection of sacks so everyone knows where the **sack races** will be after breakfast.

Have Flour Sack Races!

On your mark, get set, GO! Line them all up or take turns racing with smaller groups. Make sure each child has plenty of hopping room, so no one falls and collides with their racing neighbor. The kids love to play this game over and over! No prizes for the winners necessary — just good, classic fun!

Decorate Pancakes

Once all the kids are gathered around the pancakes and toppings, it's time to dig in. Make sure all of the toppings are in reach, so even the littlest guest can get in there and have some fun!

Food Fun and Recipes

You need a lot of pancakes for decorating and plenty of toppings to make this really fun for the kids. Pair the pancakes with mini artichoke dips and bread, healthy donuts, and a variety of milks, and you have a breakfast party worth getting out of bed for!

A variety of milks such as soy, rice, whole, and raw is a great way to offer everyone a healthy choice at the party.

WHOLE WHEAT SOUR CREAM PANCAKES WITH BLACKBERRY AGAVE SYRUP

Syrup can be made a day ahead.

syrup:
3 cups fresh blackberries
1½ cups agave nectar
juice of ½ lemon

pancakes:
1½ cups whole wheat flour
2 teaspoons baking powder
¼ teaspoon baking soda
½ teaspoon salt
3 tablespoons raw sugar
2 eggs

3 tablespoons butter, melted, plus more for greasing griddle
1⅓ cups sour cream
2 cups milk (whatever kind you prefer)

suggested pancake toppings:
• **raspberries**
• **blueberries**
• **mini chocolate chips**
• **walnuts**
• **sunflower seeds**
• **dried cherries**

Syrup: In a small saucepan, mix together blackberries, agave nectar, and lemon juice. Simmer on medium heat, stirring constantly for about 15 minutes. Cool slightly and blend to a smooth consistency.

Pancakes: In a large bowl, mix together flour, baking powder, baking soda, salt, and sugar.

In a separate bowl, mix together the eggs, melted butter, sour cream, and milk. Add wet ingredients to the dry ingredients and combine.

Heat a griddle or skillet to medium heat, add a small amount of butter to pan, and ladle batter onto the skillet to form individual pancakes. When small bubbles begin to form, the pancake is ready to flip. Cook each pancake for about 2 minutes on each side, until golden brown.

Keep pancakes warm in a low-heat oven until ready to serve. If the prepared pancakes are traveling to the party location, make them at the last minute and bring them to the party in a thermal food carrier to keep warm. Serve at the beginning of the party.

Makes 12–14 medium-size pancakes (figure at least 3 pancakes per kid) and 6 servings of syrup

Vanilla Cake Donuts with Strawberry Goop

This recipe requires donut pans.

goop:
2 cups chopped fresh strawberries
1 cup raw agave nectar

donuts:
1¼ cups all-purpose flour
½ teaspoon aluminum-free baking powder
½ teaspoon baking soda
¼ teaspoon sea salt
¼ teaspoon grated nutmeg
1 large egg
1 large egg yolk
1 cup sugar
1 packet yeast
½ cup grapeseed oil
1 teaspoon vanilla extract
½ cup sour cream

Strawberry Goop: In a small saucepan over medium heat, cook strawberries with agave nectar, stirring frequently, until the mixture becomes somewhat saucy. This should take 4-5 minutes. Set aside.

Vanilla Cake Donuts: Preheat oven to 350° F.

Sift the flour, baking powder, baking soda, salt, and nutmeg together in a large bowl. Set aside.

In the bowl of an electric mixer, mix the egg, egg yolk, sugar, and yeast on medium speed until the batter is light in color and creamy in texture.

Mix in the oil and vanilla. Add the sour cream and mix until well blended. Scrape down the sides of the bowl and mix again to make sure all ingredients are incorporated.

Add the flour mixture to the batter and mix on high until it's well blended and smooth. (There is no need to wait for the yeast to do its thing; it will react with the sugar and rise in the oven during baking.)

Pour batter into donut pan rings half to three-quarters full. (They will rise quite a bit during baking.) Bake for 12 minutes. Once baked, let the donuts cool before removing from the pan.

To serve, top donuts with strawberry goop and sift some powdered sugar, cocoa powder, or whipped cream over the top.

Makes 12 donuts

COCOA DONUTS WITH LEMON GLAZE

All donut ingredients from Vanilla Cake Donuts, plus ⅓ cup cocoa powder.

Cocoa Donuts: Use the same recipe as page 28 for the vanilla cake donut, but add ⅓ cup raw organic cocoa powder to the dry ingredients. (The raw cocoa adds a very mild chocolate flavor and color.) An awesome topping for this donut is a lemon glaze.

lemon glaze:
½ cup unsalted butter

**2 cups organic powdered sugar
  or agave powder**

4 tablespoons fresh-squeezed lemon juice

1 teaspoon grated lemon zest

Melt the butter in a saucepan and mix in the sugar, lemon juice, and zest. Whisk until smooth, remove from heat, and dip the tops of the donuts into the glaze. Let dry or consider sprinkling them with raw, organic, finely shredded coconut.

Makes 12 donuts

MINI ARTICHOKE DIPS WITH RUSTIC BREAD

You need small ramekins (3½- to 4-inch diameter) or a large muffin pan with large paper liners to make this recipe. Prepare in advance and cook just before serving.

**2 (6.5-ounce) cans artichoke hearts,
  chopped (not flavored)**

2 cups mayonnaise

3 garlic cloves, crushed

2 cups freshly grated Parmesan cheese

1 teaspoon Worcestershire sauce

1½ teaspoons wheat germ

1 teaspoon salt

pepper to taste

1 loaf of your favorite rustic bread

Preheat oven to 350°F. Coat 6 small ramekins with nonstick spray or butter or line a large muffin pan with cupcake liners.

Combine all ingredients (except for the bread) in a large bowl and mix well. Scoop into the prepared ramekins (filling them three-quarters full). Bake for 35–45 minutes, until golden brown.

Serve with slices of rustic bread for dipping.

Serves 6

Forest Faerie Dress-up Party

You're Invited . . .

to meet in the forest under the candlelit tree and whisper about the wonders of the faerie world. Dress up in silks and linens, build a faerie dwelling, and, of course, eat treats including heart-shaped summer cherry pie pops!

The Inspiration

Girls LOVE faeries! Who doesn't love the idea of a cute little something flying about with gorgeous wings and wearing a silk spun dress? A warm spring afternoon or evening just screams for a faerie party in the forest. Faeries are about believing in something that we may not be able to see but LOVE the idea of.

PROJECTS AND MATERIALS

Printed fabric invitations
- printable pieces of cream-colored fabric (available at art supply stores)
- computer with word processing program and color printer
- twig or natural stick
- string or twine

Felted faeirie wands
- all-wool flat felt (any color)
- dowel or natural stick
- ribbons
- wool fleece or premade wool ball

Tree decor
- pom-pom yarn
- glitter leaves and decorative butterflies
- scissors
- hot glue and hot glue gun
- large stick to hang from a tree
- 8 recycled glass jars
- 8 small votive candles
- sand
- wire and wire cutters

Table decor
- old-fashioned linens in a soft color palette (try white and cream tones)
- tin cans to use as flower vases
- old books or photo album
- pictures of faeries

Dress-up
- girly dresses
- clothespins (to hang dresses) or an old trunk (alternatively, you can ask the girls to bring special dress-up dresses to add to the collection for the day)

Faerie dwellings
- small elements from nature such as sticks, acorns, feathers, pebbles, shells, and pinecones
- glass beads and scraps of fabric

Recipes
- Deliciously Sweet and Savory Cheesy Panini with Maple Bacon
- Cheesy Faerie Wands and Olive Bar with Chocolate Raisins
- Heart-shaped Cherry-Strawberry Pie Pops and Mini Pies

TIMELINE

2 weeks prior to event:
- choose your location
- create invites and hand them out

1 week prior to event:
- gather table decor and dishware
- make elements for hanging forest chandelier
- make felted wool faerie wands
- make pom-pom hanging pretties
- gather dresses for dress-up (borrow, borrow, borrow!!)
- print out a menu
- print out pictures of faeries

Day prior to event:
- make pie pops and mini pies
- make base for the faerie dwelling
- make cheese wands

Day of event:
- make paninis immediately before setting out for party location
- set up food table and hang forest chandelier
- hang dress-up dresses in a tree with clothespins or lay in a trunk
- locate a special spot to put the faerie dwelling; place decorating and building elements nearby

Create Invitations

- Using your computer's word porcessing program, find a fun font and color, create a simple text document that gives the details of your party and include a hand-drawn or copyright-free image that matches your theme.

- Print out the invitation on the fabric paper and glue a stick to the top of the invite, folding the fabric over on the top. The stick should be slightly longer than the width of the fabric so that it sticks out on either end.

- Tie a string to the two ends of the stick so it can hang like a small banner.

- Hand-deliver these special invitations to the lucky girls invited!

Make Felted Wool Flower Faerie Wands as Giveaways

If you want the girls to take home a special gift to remind them of the day, consider making simple felted flower faerie wands. For a very simple version, tie multiple ribbons to sticks and skip the flower at the top. To make a slightly more elaborate wand:

- Cut petal shapes out of the flat felted wool.

- Cut one 1½-inch circle as the center "anchor."

- Organize the petals around the circle to make a flower shape.

- Hand- or machine-sew the petals onto the circle with the points touching and overlapping in the middle.

- Wet-felt a ball for the visible part of the center by rolling and massaging wet soapy wool fleece in the palms of your hands, or purchase a premade wool ball, or use a button for the center. Sew the center to the front of the anchor circle.

- Sew ribbons onto the anchor circle and glue the flower to a wood dowel (you can leave this natural or paint it) or a natural stick. After gluing, you may want to give it a safety stitch to be sure the flower stays on the wand after hours of exuberant faerie activity!

Set the Scene

Choose a beautiful natural location such as a **forest or a park** (that won't be too crowded) or a backyard. Ideally the space offers the opportunity for the girls to run and twirl and gather sticks and flowers. Decorate your faerie space with recycled and upcylced eco-friendly goodies!

Use pom-pom yarn (available at craft stores) and glitter leaves and butterflies to make **hanging decorations for the trees**. Cut a long piece of pom-pom yarn and hot glue a pretty element to the end of it.

To create **a forest chandelier**, find a loose, broken branch that you can hang from an attached (live) tree branch at your location. Hang the loose branch with sturdy string at either end. Place a small amount of sand in the bottom of several recycled glass jars and add a small votive candle to each jar. (Adding sand to the bottom of the jar keeps the candle in place and prevents the melted wax from sticking to the bottom of the jar.) Wrap thick wire (sold at a craft store in the jewelry section) around the top rim of the jar and twist it around the top of the jar. Continue to bend and twist the wire until you have it tightly and securely wrapped around the jar. Attach a separate piece of wire to either side of the neck wire and twist this wire over the top of the jar to create a handle. Once you get the hang of this, it will take about 5 minutes per jar. Attach this top loop to sturdy string and tie the string to the suspended branch. Do this with several jars and you'll have a magical-looking forest chandelier.

Cover a table with old-fashioned linens. I used borrowed crocheted table covers and real linens for the tabletop and accented it with old boxes, recycled tin cans to use as vases, freshly picked flowers from the garden, antique spoons, and real wineglasses! Girls feel SO special drinking out of wineglasses! (You can often find glasses for super cheap at the thrift store. Mismatched styles only add flair!) Place an old book on the table or an antique photo album (also a possible thrift store item). Put old pictures of faeries in the album for the girls to look at while they were sitting around the table.

Gather "dress-up" dresses from friends or the girls invited and also ask them to bring a few extra items of their own to share with others. Girls especially love silk dresses and have fun with silk wings, too!

Build Faerie Dwellings

Build a faerie dwelling with collected nature objects and some premade goodies as a random act of beauty!

Before the party use sticks, acorns, feathers, glass beads, and scraps of fabric to create a faerie dwelling that the girls can build upon when they get there. Alternatively, you can have them build the entire faerie house from found natural objects and special accents you may bring along.

In order to begin a faerie dwelling at home, we used sticks, scraps of fabric, little glass beads, tiny rocks, and bits of string. We glued these items together to create a little tepee-style dwelling. Keep the structure simple so the girls will be inspired to continue the decorating and building at the party. Once at the party location, place the faerie structure alongside a lovely tree and let the girls began to bring it to life with rose petals, sparkle beads, flowers, feathers, shells, sticks, and moss. Leave the faerie dwelling (or dwellings) in place for others to find and enjoy, but make sure to take home any non-natural items at the end of the party as we would not want our forest friends to accidentally be hurt by them. If you want to leave everything in place at the party's end, use only natural elements found in the area.

Food Fun and Recipes

As it is likely the little faeries will be running around, it's great to have foods that they can throw in their baskets as they are fluttering by the food table. Cheesy paninis with maple bacon are amazing with their sweet and savory flavors, faerie cheese puffed wands stay within your theme, and heart-shaped pie pops and mini pies are the perfect girly treat.

Note: A nice lemon-flavored iced tea is a great drink to serve on a hot day while faeries are afoot!

DELICIOUSLY SWEET AND SAVORY CHEESY PANINI WITH MAPLE BACON

This recipe requires a panini grill or press. The amounts listed are for 1 full sandwich. Make enough for about half a sandwich per child.

- **2 slices turkey bacon**
- **1 tablespoon of pure maple syrup**
- **2 slices sourdough bread**
- **2 slices Havarti cheese**

Heat a panini grill or sandwich press.

Place bacon in a 2-inch-deep baking dish, and baste with maple syrup.

Put the bacon in a cold oven, turn on to 375°F, and bake for 15–18 minutes.

Using a pastry brush, brush the inside of each piece of bread with maple syrup.

Add cheese slices and cooked turkey bacon.

Place on your panini press, and grill for about 3 minutes on each side.

Cut in half and serve warm.

CHEESY FAERIE WANDS AND OLIVE BAR WITH CHOCOLATE RAISINS

cornstarch for dusting baking sheet

flour for dusting work surface

1 package puff pastry dough, thawed

1 egg, beaten

1 tablespoon unsalted butter, melted

½ cup freshly grated Parmesan cheese

1 tablespoon poppy seeds

mixed olives

chocolate-covered raisins

Preheat oven to 400°F. Lightly dust a baking sheet with cornstarch and set aside.

Roll out puff pastry on lightly floured surface. Brush top surface with egg and melted butter.

Press Parmesan cheese and poppy seeds into the surface of the dough.

With a pizza cutter, slice long strips of the dough. Twist each strip and place on prepared baking sheet.

Bake for 10–12 minutes, until golden brown. Remove, let cool, and store in an airtight container.

Arrange olives, chocolate-covered raisins, and cheese wands on the eating table. You could also add jam and cheese if you wish.

Makes 12–15 wands

HEART-SHAPED CHERRY-STRAWBERRY PIE POPS AND MINI PIES

You'll need short cardboard lollipop sticks for the pie pops.

filling:
- 1 ½ tablespoons unsalted butter
- 1 cup pitted and halved fresh Bing cherries
- 1 cup halved fresh strawberries
- 1 cup raw agave nectar
- juice and zest of 1 whole lemon
- ¼ teaspoon vanilla extract
- 1 pinch sea salt
- 1 tablespoon arrowroot

pie crust:
- 1 ⅓ cups all-purpose unbleached flour, plus more for coating work surface
- 2 pinches pure cane sugar
- 1 pinch salt
- 8 tablespoons (1 stick) unsalted butter, cut into pieces
- ½ cup ice-cold water
- 1 egg beaten with a little water, for egg wash

Filling: In a saucepan, over medium heat, melt butter. Add cherries, strawberries, agave nectar, lemonjuice and zest, vanilla, and salt. Mix together for about 5 minutes, until the cherries start to form a liquid. Turn heat down to low.

Add the arrowroot, and mix until a bit thicker, about 3 minutes. The filling should be the consistency of jam or paste — not too runny. You may add a bit more arrowroot if you prefer a thicker filling.

Remove from stovetop and set aside until pie crust is prepared.

Pie crust: In the large bowl of a standing mixer, put flour, sugar, and salt, and lightly mix together with your hand.

Using the dough hook on low to medium speed, start to drop in the butter pieces, slowly adding water as you are dropping in butter pieces, until both are fully incorporated. This will be a sticky dough.

Place dough on a floured surface and roll out until about ¼ inch thick.

Preheat oven to 350°F.

Using a round cookie cutter, or other 4- to 5-inch diameter cutter, cut out shapes from the rolled dough.

Put a small amount of pie filling (about 1 tablespoon) directly in the center of half the cutout dough shapes. Place a pop stick on top of the filling, and press it down through the filling and into the bottom dough. Leave some filled bases without a stick; those will be the mini pies.

Place matching cutout shape on top of each filled base and press the edges together with wet fingers. Using a clean pop stick or the tines of a fork, make indentations around the pie pop edges. Make small, shallow slits on the top surface of the pie pop with a knife, but don't slice all the way through the dough.

Brush egg wash on top of each pie or pop with a pastry brush. Place them on a baking sheet lined with parchment paper. Cook in the oven for about 15 minutes, until golden brown on top. Remove from oven and cool on a wire rack. Store in an airtight glass container and serve at room temperature.

Makes 12–15 mini pies or pie pops

Sun-kissed Summer

Welcome to Summer! Summer brings a time of bonfires, dancing, bike riding, playing music, and honoring the sun as crops grow and bloom. Summer solstice is on or near June 21 and is the longest day of the year. Summer is a time when kids run free and splash through sprinklers; we make room for blow-up pools and ocean tides; and dirt-caked kids come in from days filled with play. Picnics are had, lemonade stands are built, and a whole $2.00 is made in one short afternoon. So grab your bathing suit and bask in the light of long days and super-fun parties!

The fun of Summer is…

sipping ice-cold *lemonade*;

splashing in the **ocean** searching for sea shells;

eating **watermelon** and ice pops;

watching fireworks explode in the sky;

enjoying **campouts** and *strawberry* picking;

the promise of soft, warm evenings filled

with fireflies and **carnival** rides …

~MENU~

grilled FLATBREAD PIZZAS with
fun *toppings*

bbq HERBED CHICKEN

roasted *summer* baby CARROTS

grilled PEACH + BLACKBERRY granola
parfaits with *fresh lemon vanilla* whipped
cream

Summer Solstice Beach Party

You're Invited...

to spend the afternoon at the beach! Get sandy while looking for sea glass, eating BBQ, digging under the smile tent, and building a sweet dessert from the grilled peach parfait bar. Splash around with friends in the warm waves of summer!

The Inspiration

Summer solstice, the longest day of the year, is a fun and playful holiday and a perfect reason to gather friends on the beach to play together until the warm evening breezes hit. This party is the perfect way to officially kick off the summer!

PROJECTS AND MATERIALS

Watercolored invitations
- watercolor paper and paints
- paintbrushes
- computer and color printer
- sea stars (starfish)
- hot glue gun and glue sticks

Seashell hanging garland
- hemp rope or twine
- various shells and sea stars
- hot glue gun and glue sticks

Smile tent and outside decor
- repurposed piece of wood
- white and aqua nontoxic paints
- a course sandpaper
- white shells
- hot glue gun and glue sticks
- large poles and large pieces of fabric to make a tent
- drill
- sturdy twine or hemp cord

Table decor
- white tablecloth
- recycled glass bottles with cloth napkins rubber-banded around them with forks placed on the side under the rubber bands
- extra shells and sea stars
- canning jars with sand and a votive candle in them
- printed menu to place on the table

Sea glass hunt and necklace making
- sea glass
- buckets to collect sea glass and shells
- bendable necklace wire
- scissors and wire cutters
- hemp or string to hang necklaces

Recipes
- BBQ Sesame Chicken and Roasted Summer Carrots
- Grilled Flatbread Pizzas
- Grilled Peach, Blackberry, and Granola Parfaits with Lemon-Vanilla Whipped Cream

TIMELINE

2 weeks prior to event:
- choose your beach spot
- create invites and hand them out

1 week prior to event:
- gather table decor and start recycling glass bottles to use for drinking cups
- make seashell hanging garland
- make inspirational smile sign out of shells
- gather sea glass, wire, and scissors for the beach craft

Day prior to event:
- gather toppings and prep them for the grilled flatbreads

Day of event:
- make whipped cream
- set up smile tent and food table
- hang seashell garland
- set up peach parfait bar
- BBQ food at the beach

SEASIDE PLAY

COME + HANG OUT WITH US FOR...

bbq GOODIES

sea glass hunt + necklace making

SMILE *hut*

Sand castle construction

general beach MAYHEM

2PM LEO CARILLO MALIBU BEACH
GO TO THE SMILE HUT AT THE BOTTOM OF THE STAIRS

Create Invitations

- Have your child watercolor paper in turquoise and green tones. This paper will go through your printer, so choose paper size and thickness accordingly. Set painted papers aside to dry.

- Prepare the invitations using a computer word processing program. Use various fonts in different weights and sizes, and include all the details of your party. Arrange the information on only a portion of the page; you will reduce the page size after printing.

- Feed the painted watercolor paper through a color printer and print out the invitations.

- Tear around the edges of the invitations to make them smaller and create soft edges. Hot glue a small sea star to each invitation.

- Hand-deliver invitations to your lucky guests.

Set the Scene

Choose a **beach** spot that you love and that isn't typically crowded during the day of the week and time you plan to host the party.

Half-fill small canning jars with sand and place **votive candles** and a few seashells into the sand. Place a couple of these small candle holders on the table.

Wrap recycled glass bottles with **turquoise-blue cloth napkins** and use a rubber band to hold them in place. Add a fork to each bottle place setting by slipping it under the rubber band. Cluster together these standing place settings on your table.

Prepare a **tabletop menu board** using cardstock and a computer and printer. List all your party foods. Once printed, embellish your tabletop menu board with sticks and shells.

The table: Bring a fold-up table that you can cover with a white tablecloth and decorate with all of your tableware, candles, standing place settings, and menu board.

Make a seashell garland: Cut a piece of thick hemp rope or twine about 1 feet long. Using more twine in varying lengths, hang sea stars from the main rope by wrapping a sea star arm with twine and tying it in place along the main length of twine. Cut a few more varying lengths of twine and, using a hot glue gun, glue several small shells along each piece of twine. Intersperse these long glued shell twine pieces with sea star dangles to give the garland different lengths throughout. Hang the shell garland from the front of the table.

Create a "smile" sign: Find an old piece of wood, sand it with coarse sand paper, and paint the board white. Once completely dry, cover with another layer of paint, this time aqua. After paint has dried, use the sandpaper to rough up the paint and make the board appear old or weather-worn. Hot glue the word SMILE in shells on the board. Drill two holes, one in each top corner, and tie sturdy twine or hemp cord through each one, leaving enough extra cord to be able to hang the sign.

Once at the beach, **build a makeshift tent** by pushing poles in the sand and draping white fabric (sheets work well) to create a top and sides. Tie the sign's cords to the poles or use sturdy clips to hang the smile sign above the tent. The children can take pictures with their friends under the sign and also use the space as a spot to stay out of the sun for a bit.

Beach Play: Sea Glass Hunt and Necklace Making

Bring sea glass (naturally smoothed by the surf is lovely, but machine-tumbled is less expensive and easier to come by) to the beach and spread it around the sand in a designated area for the children to find. You can also encourage the children to find shells and rocks and share the found treasures with each other. Once all the treasure is collected, let each child choose a favorite piece of sea glass with which to make a wire-wrapped pendant necklace. Depending on the age of the children attending, adults may need to be more (for younger children) or less (for older children) hands-on with this project.

To make the sea glass pendant, begin with a long piece of bendable necklace wire in whatever thickness you prefer. The wire (available at bead shops or craft stores in the jewelry-making supply aisle) is very pliable and easy to bend using only your hands, so no special tools are required. Begin wrapping the piece of wire around the sea glass pendant in a decorative way. Make sure to secure the sea glass with the wire so it will not slide out, but don't obscure too much of the pendant. Bend a loop at the top of the pendant and loop the wire around the base of the loop to secure it in place. Thread a cord through the top loop, and tie the necklace around the child's neck. If any wires are sticking out of the final piece, you can use small wire cutters to clip the ends or tuck it under another piece of wire.

These keepsakes can be taken home by the children as their own creation and remembrance of the fun summer day they had.

Food Fun and Recipes

A summer party needs delicious goodies and hosting a BBQ is a great way to enjoy hot food at the beach. You will need to bring a grill or make sure that the beach has one readily available. You'll also need to bring a large cooler to keep the marinating chicken cold and the whipped cream chilled.

BBQ SESAME CHICKEN AND ROASTED SUMMER CARROTS

chicken:

½ cup roasted sesame oil

1 tablespoon sesame seeds

½ cup teriyaki sauce

juice of 1 lemon

salt and pepper to taste

1 whole free-range chicken

carrots:

1 tablespoon unsalted butter

2 cloves garlic

10–12 large carrots with greens on

salt and pepper to taste

Arrange charcoal in a pile in the center of the grill well and preheat for about 20 minutes.

While grill is preheating, prepare and marinate the chicken: Combine sesame oil, sesame seeds, teriyaki sauce, lemon juice, and salt and pepper to taste. Marinate chicken in the sauce in a container in a cooler for approximately 20 minutes.

When grill is heated, place chicken directly on the grill, brush with any remaining sauce, and cook for 50 minutes, until juices run clear. Once fully cooked, set aside in a large pot to keep warm until ready to eat.

In a small pot on the grill, melt butter. Add garlic cloves and sauté for 3–4 minutes. Pour garlic butter over the raw cleaned carrots (greens still in place), sprinkle with salt and pepper to taste, and place directly on the hot grill. Grill carrots for about 15 minutes. Serve warm alongside the chicken.

Serves 5

GRILLED FLATBREAD PIZZAS

You'll need a round baking sheet to cook the flatbreads.

pizza:
- **3–4 10-inch whole wheat flatbread crusts**
- **4 cups favorite pizza sauce**

toppings:
- **1 cup crumbled feta cheese**
- **2 cups shredded mozzarella cheese**
- **1 cup sliced olives**
- **1 cup chopped sun-dried tomatoes**
- **1 cup sliced red onions**

Place baking sheet on grill for 1 minute to heat up before adding flatbread.

Spread each flatbread with sauce and add toppings in desired combinations.

Place prepared flatbread pizzas (one at a time or however many will fit) on the baking sheet to cook.

Grill for about 8–10 minutes, until cheese melts and toppings cook down. Remove from the grill, slice, and serve warm.

Serves 8

GRILLED PEACH, BLACKBERRY, AND GRANOLA PARFAITS WITH LEMON-VANILLA WHIPPED CREAM

You'll need to make the Lemon-Vanilla Whipped Cream in advance and carry it to the party location in a cooler.

whipped cream:

2 cups heavy whipping cream

I cup raw agave nectar

juice of I lemon

2 tablespoons vanilla extract

parfait:

8 peaches, cut into quarters

I cup honey

I package bamboo skewers

2 cups your favorite granola

2 cups fresh blackberries

To make the Lemon-Vanilla Whipped Cream, pour the whipping cream in the large bowl of an electric mixer and whip on medium speed for about 4–5 minutes, until the cream reaches a whipped and firm consistency. Add agave nectar, lemon juice, and vanilla extract. Mix for another 4–5 minutes, until it's frothy like whipped cream. Taste for sweetness and add additional sweetener if desired. Refrigerate until ready to serve.

Once you're at the beach and the party is in full swing, you can prepare the remaining parfait ingredients.

Brush cut peaches with honey. Place peach wedges on bamboo skewers and place directly on a hot grill for 4–5 minutes, until the peaches have softened. Remove from grill and place on a platter.

Set the remaining parfait ingredients out on a table so individuals can put together their own parfaits. To prepare the parfaits, fill the bottom of each canning jar cup with a layer of granola, followed by a layer of whipped cream and then blackberries. Continue to layer ingredients into the jars in that order until jars are full. Top with a dollop of whipped cream and a blackberry. Serve with still warm grilled peaches to dip into the parfaits or mound on the top.

Serves 8

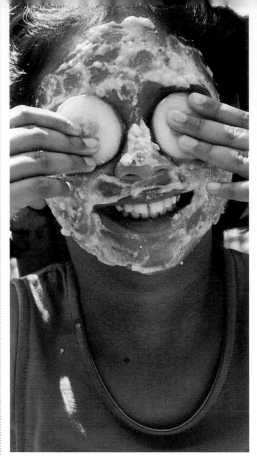

Grapefruit SugarScrub

Natural Spa Party

You're Invited…

to spend the afternoon lounging with the girls, getting pampered with chocolate facials, grapefruit sugar scrubs, and lluxurious foot soaks, while snacking on refreshing Italian ices, hearty quesadillas, mini fruit tarts, and cookies. Now that is an afternoon well spent!

The Inspiration

Who doesn't love a little pampering once in a while? The Natural Spa Party was inspired by my very girly daughter, Lotus, who loves a daily foot rub and my recipe for chocolate facials. Her girlfriends enjoy playing spa and this party is a relaxing few hours filled with pretty colors, good food, and natural "edible" products.

PROJECTS AND MATERIALS

Watercolored invitations
- watercolor paper and paints
- paintbrushes
- computer and color printer
- wooden sticks
- hot glue gun and glue sticks
- small, fresh roses and a silk ribbon
- digital photograph of each invitee

"Pamper Me" hanging sign
- rope or twine
- 8 pieces of paper (in color theme of reds/pinks/yellows/oranges) to print out the words "Pamper me"
- torn strips of fabric (from old shirts or dresses) in colors that match your party theme
- wooden clothespins

Table decor
- white tablecloth and colored cloth napkins
- pink and yellow flowers for the tables
- recycled glass jars to hold flowers
- cardstock (for spa elements identification labels)
- 5 containers for spa products plus spoons for each

Other decor
- small chair for foot-soak station
- large container for foot soak
- "girls are beautiful" printed sign

Natural Spa Recipes
- Chocolate Facial
- Banana and Avocado Face Mask
- Grapefruit Sugar Scrub
- Lavender and Rose Petal Foot Soak
- Apricot Brown Sugar Sugar Scrub
- Rosemary and Mint Sea Salt Bath Mix

Recipes
- Black Bean, Corn, and Cheese Quesadillas with Blue Corn Chips
- Sweet and Savory Strawberry and Apricot Tarts
- Italian Ices with Lemon-Vanilla Pizzelles

TIMELINE

2 weeks prior to event:
- choose your home spa location
- acquire digital photos of invitees
- create and deliver invitations

I week prior to event:
- gather table decor, dishware for spa products, and recycled glass bottles for flower vases
- make "pamper me" banner
- make product identification labels
- make "girls r beautiful" sign

Day prior to event:
- gather rose petals and place in a baggie in the refrigerator
- make pizzelle cookies
- make Italian ices so they have plenty of time to freeze before the party
- make all spa treatments (except foot soak), cover tightly, and refrigerate

Day of event:
- set up spa table and food table
- hang "pamper me" sign
- hang "girls r beautiful" sign
- make lavender and rose petal foot soak
- sliced cocumbers for eye covers

Create Invitations

- Have your child watercolor paper in pink, orange, and yellow tones. This paper will go through your printer, so choose paper size and thickness accordingly. Set painted papers aside to dry.

- Prepare the individualized invitations using a computer word processing program. For each invite, insert the digital picture of the child invited with her name (large) in a fun font of your choice. Then add the details of the party.

- Do not feel the need to fill the full page; you can reduce the paper size after printing. Select colors for the type that work with the watercolor backgrounds already painted on the paper.

- Feed the painted watercolor paper through a color printer and print out your invitations.

- Tear around the edges of the invites to make the page smaller and create soft edges. Hot glue the paper invitation to a long stick (like a lollipop).

- On the day you deliver the invitations, tie small roses or other flowers to the base of the invite (where it meets the stick) with a ribbon or a torn piece of fabric from an upcycled dress.

Set the Scene

Choose a spot to host your Natural Spa Party, such as a **comfortable backyard** or a **pool with lounge chairs.**

Use a **white tablecloth** and cloth napkins in pinks, oranges, and yellows. Wrap glass jars or bottles with strips of fabric and fill with fresh flowers that match your colors such as baby pink roses and yellow peonies.

Make a **"Pamper Me" banner:** Type out the words "Pamper Me," in large type (one letter per page), in a fun font in a word processing document, and print out each letter on a separate piece of color paper. Use wooden clothespins to hang each printed letter page from a rope or twine hanging near your party spot. For extra color, tie strips of fabric (torn from an old shirt or dress that matches the color theme) between letters on the sign.

Print out a **"Girls R Beautiful" sign:** Type "Girls R Beautiful" into a word processing document and print it out on a piece of paper that matches your color theme. Hang this simple sign anywhere at the party to emphasize the theme that all girls are special and beautiful, inside and out!

Create a **spa products bar:** Have a special table at the party designated just for the spa products. You can direct the girls to the natural spa bar for their pampering treatments. Make simple identification cards, either by writing them out by hand or printing them from your computer, for each spa product.

Create a **foot-soak station:** Make the lavender and rose petal foot soak and create an area where the girls will go to soak their feet. Depending on the number or girls attending, you may wish to have more than one soak container available at a time.

Make Natural Spa Products

Create all of the spa recipes (except the foot soak) a day before the party so everything is ready to use at the event. There is a lot to do the day before this party. You may want to call in helping hands. Don't forget to have some cucumbers ready for slicing into rounds for eye covers — they really complete the look. Use the Rosemary and Mint Sea Salt Bath Mix recipe to create simple giveaways for the girls as a remembrance of the day. Each spa product recipe below makes enough for about 8 girls.

CHOCOLATE FACIAL

½ cup cocoa powder

4 tablespoons oats

½ cup honey

3 teaspoons cottage cheese

½ cup fresh plain yogurt

Mix all ingredients together, cover, and refrigerate until ready to use.

Apply to face and leave on for 10 minutes or until girls want to eat it off! Rinse off with water.

BANANA AND AVOCADO FACE MASK

2 bananas, mashed

1 ripe avocado, mashed

½ cup plain yogurt

1 tablespoon flaxseed

1 tablespoon honey

1 tablespoon almond oil

Mix all ingredients together, cover, and refrigerate until ready to use.

Apply to face and leave on for 10–15 minutes. Rinse off with water.

GRAPEFRUIT SUGAR SCRUB

2 cups pure cane sugar

1 cup almond oil

2 whole grapefruits, squeezed

1 grapefruit, zested

1 tablespoon grapefruit essential oil

Mix all ingredients together, cover, and refrigerate until ready to use.

Apply to hands and feet and scrub into skin. Enjoy the amazing scent. Rinse off with water.

APRICOT BROWN SUGAR SCRUB

10–12 apricots, chopped

¼ cup honey

¼ cup water

2 cups brown sugar

½ cup almond oil

Place chopped apricots in a large pot. Add honey and water. Boil for approximately 10–12 minutes or until soft. Remove pot from stove and let cool.

Puree cooled apricot mix, then add remaining ingredients and mix. Cover and refrigerate until ready to use.

LAVENDER AND ROSE PETAL FOOT SOAK

10 cups warm water

2 tablespoons lavender essential oil

2 cups fresh rose petals

1 tablespoon peppermint essential oil

Mix all ingredients together and put in large container for the girls to be able to soak their feet. Soak feet until soft!

ROSEMARY AND MINT SEA SALT BATH MIX

5 cups coarse sea salt

2 sprigs fresh rosemary

1 tablespoon peppermint essential oil

Mix all the ingredients together, put into individual canning jars, and tie up with a matching ribbon from the banner ties. Hand out to each girl at the party to take home as a goodie from the party.

Food Fun and Recipes

The Natural Spa Party needs easy-to-eat foods that the girls can carry around with them while enjoying various treatments. Quesadillas are perfect, and the girls can even eat them while they have their facial masks on! Follow them up with bite-size tarts, Italian ices, and pizzelle cookies, and you have the makings for a comforting and joyful afternoon!

BLACK BEAN, CORN, AND CHEESE QUESADILLAS

10 whole wheat tortillas

2 cups cooked black beans

1 cup Organic corn kernels

2 cups grated cheese (e.g., mixed cheddar and Monterey Jack cheese)

butter (optional)

4 avocados, sliced, on the side

blue corn chips and favorite salsa on the side

Line up 5 tortillas on a cutting board.

Add black beans, corn, and cheese to each one, then top each one with another tortilla (think tortilla sandwich).

Heat skillet to medium-hot, and place one completed quesadilla in the pan. (Note: You can add a little butter to the pan, but it is not needed.) Cook quesadilla on the first side for about 3 minutes, then carefully flip it over so the ingredients do not fall out. Let the next side cook for about 3 minutes, and flip again. Continue flipping the quesadilla until it is crisp and golden brown on both sides. Remove and keep warm.

Repeat with the other quesadillas. When all quesadillas are cooked, cut each one into 4 easy-to-hold slices. Serve warm. Offer avovado sliced, blue corn chips, and salsa as accompaniments.

Serves 5

SWEET AND SAVORY STRAWBERRY AND APRICOT TARTS

Make these in a mini cupcake pan. They can be made a day ahead and served at room temperature.

10 fresh apricots, chopped into pieces

2 cups chopped fresh strawberries

½ cup honey + ¼ cup honey for drizzle

½ cup raw agave nectar

1 sheet puff pastry, chilled, but not frozen

4 tablespoons (½ stick) butter, melted

1 cup chopped pistachios

½ cup shredded spicy cheese (your favorite variety)

Preheat oven to 350°F. Spray a nonstick mini cupcake pan with cooking spray.

In a large pot, combine apricots and strawberries. Add ½ cup honey and agave nectar, then boil down for approximately 10–12 minutes until fruit is soft. Remove from stove and let cool. Then puree in a blender or food processor and set aside.

Roll out the puff pastry on a floured surface and, using a 4- to 5-inch round cookie cutter, cut circles from the dough. Brush each dough circle with melted butter.

Press the circles into the mini cupcake pan, with the edges pressing up the sides, forming a cup of puff pastry. Lightly poke the bottom of each one with a fork.

Line each puff pastry shell with a layer of chopped pistachios, then add a dollop of the apricot-strawberry puree, and sprinkle some spicy cheese on top of that. End with another layer of chopped pistachios.

Drizzle with honey and bake for 15–18 minutes until pastry has puffed up and is light and golden brown in color.

Serves 10 (about 20 mini tarts)

LEMON-VANILLA PIZZELLES

You will need a pizzelle maker to make this recipe. Prepare the pizzelles the day before the party.

2 cups all-purpose flour	5 tablespoons butter, melted and cooled
1 tablespoon baking powder	3 teaspoons pure vanilla extract
¾ cup sugar	2 lemons, juiced
¼ teaspoon ground cinnamon	1 lemon, zested
3 eggs	fresh raspberries, as garnish

In a medium bowl, mix together flour, baking powder, sugar, and cinnamon. Set aside.

In a large bowl, beat the eggs until well whipped. Add butter, vanilla, lemon juice, and lemon zest.

Beat to combine.

Add dry ingredients and use hand-held mixer on medium to beat batter until smooth.

Heat electric pizzelle iron according to manufacturer's directions.

For each pizzelle, place a tablespoon of batter on pizzelle iron. Close lid, and bake according to manufacturer's directions. Turn pizzelles out onto a paper towel to cool. Repeat with remaining batter. Store cooled pizzelles in an airtight container until ready to serve.

Serve garnished with fresh raspberries.

Makes about 20 pizzelles

Italian Ices

Make these a day or two in advance so they have time to freeze. You will need small paper cups for freezing them.

2 pints fresh raspberries

4⅛ cups (25 ounces) sparkling grapefruit juice

1 pint fresh blackberries

4⅛ cups (25 ounces) sparkling pomegranate juice

½ honeydew, peeled and cubed

4⅛ cups (25 ounces) sparkling clementine juice

1 lemon (to wet the rim of serving glasses)

½ cup raw sugar (to rim glasses)

Combine raspberries with sparkling grapefruit juice in a blender and mix until well blended. Pour into paper cups and freeze.

Combine blackberries with sparkling pomegranate juice in a blender and mix until well blended. Pour into paper cups and freeze.

Combine honeydew melon pieces with sparkling clementine juice in a blender and mix until well blended. Pour into paper cups and freeze.

Immediately before serving, tear open the paper cups and chop the frozen ices into shaved ice consistency. Use a lemon to wet the rim of individual glasses and dip in raw sugar to coat the rim. Transfer to clear glasses. Serve immediately.

Makes 12–15 servings

BERRY CHECK IN

Strawberry-Picking and Jam-Making Party

You're Invited...

to spend the day picking the freshest, sweetest organic berries you can find. Meet at the farm and enjoy a simple lunch of turkey wraps, pickles, homemade or purchased buttermilk biscuits and jam, strawberry ice cream, and a splash of homemade lemonade before heading out with your basket and friends for a berry-picking great time. Then head back to the kitchen to create the perfect summertime jam.

The Inspiration

Children love berries, and what better way to celebrate the season than to come together for a berry-picking and jam-making party? A possible hayride around the farm or an impromptu jam music session will make it even better. A party at the farm is always a special gathering, and no one ever leaves empty-handed. Then you get to turn those berries into a delicious jam that can be used all summer long!

PROJECTS AND MATERIALS

Strawberry container invitations
- pint-size cardboard strawberry container
- fresh strawberries
- notecard or cardstock label
- fine-point marker
- tape

Outside decor
- a U-Pick berry farm with all the amenities (big, red barn; open space; rows of ripe berries; old wagon; wooden crates; hay bundles; etc.)

Watercolored "Strawberry-Picking Party" banner
- watercolor paper
- watercolor paint and brushes
- hole punch
- marker pen
- silk ribbon

Table decor
- vintage enamel pie plates as dishware
- canning jars (or enamel cups) for drinks
- eclectic old silverware and measuring spoons to eat with

Field use
- spray bottles
- fresh mint and rosemary, lemon slices, essential oils
- galvanized tin bucket or tub
- baskets (to use when berry picking)
- strips of colorful recycled fabric

Recipes
- Strawberry-Orange Jam (requires some canning supplies)
- Ginger-Mint Lemonade
- Wheat Turkey Wraps

TIMELINE

2 weeks to 1 month prior to event:
- choose a farm and call ahead to make reservations. Inquire about all of the different types of berries that might be ready for picking
- if possible, reserve a tractor or hayride for all of the children, and ask if there is an area you can set up for your picnic spot
- create invitations and deliver them to guests
- prepare vanilla sugar for jam

1 week prior to event:
- gather together all table and outdoor decor
- make banner

Day prior to event:
- make Ginger-Mint Lemonade
- bake or purchase biscuits
- gather and clean jam-making materials

Day of event:
- make Wheat Turkey Wraps
- place water bottles at the end of each picking row
- setup picnic area
- sterilize jars and make jam

Create Invitations

• Buy baskets of strawberries and a handful of pint-size cardboard berry containers. You may be able to get these classic berry containers from your local farmer at the U-Pick farm where you will hold your party, or from the farmer at the farmers' market if you are buying berries.

• On a fun card or cardboard label, handwrite the invitation details. Depending on the type of card you use, write the party details inside or on the back of the card.

• Adhere the label to the strawberry basket with tape so your guests can easily remove it.

• Hand-deliver these tempting, scrumptious strawberry basket invitations to your guests.

Set the Scene

A **U-Pick berry farm** is an ideal place to hold a party with minimal extra decor. (Begin your search for the perfect farm at www.pickyourown.org.) Almost every farm has a hayride or other fun activities to enjoy. You can gather the children and find a nice spot to set up and enjoy a **picnic-style lunch**. You can also use a set of wooden crates, or an old wagon in the middle of the field by some shady trees to set up your party picnic.

Have your guests bring a basket to collect their berries in, or gather a collection of baskets from thrift stores for them. Provide torn fabric and clothing to use to **decorate the rim of the baskets**, which is both a fun activity as well as a great way to identify each child's baskets.

Use enamel pie plates for **simple lunch decor**. (These are often available at thrift stores.) They lend a rustic feel to the party, while being nonbreakable and fun for children to eat on. Use canning jars for drinking glasses.

Make a "strawberry-picking party" **watercolored banner**. Have your child paint sheets of water-color paper with fun colors. When the paint is completely dry, cut paper into 22 (approximately 4 x 6-inch) pieces. Write the words "strawberry picking party" on the papers, one letter per sheet. Use a hole punch to make two holes near the top of each card, and then string the full word together with a long silk ribbon. Hang the sign between two trees or fence posts.

While berry picking is a fun activity for children, it can also be a hot one. **Fill small spray bottles** with a combination of water, mint, rosemary, lemon, and various essential oils to give them refreshing smells. Gather a few of these bottles in a galvanized tin bucket, either at the end of the picking row or at the picnic spot, and encourage children to use them as often as needed. They become a fun party toy!

Make Strawberry-Orange Jam

Gathering together children to pick strawberries is a wonderful excuse for a party, but adding in making their own jam takes the party up a notch. The party will likely have to be transported from the U-Pick farm back to your kitchen for this step, but having a jar of homemade jam to take home is very much worth the effort.

Have children wash the berries in a tub outdoors while the water for sterilizing the jars is boiling on the stovetop inside. Mashing the fruit in a big tin bucket outside is fun and a great way to get all the kids involved in the jam-making process. Be sure to make enough jars of jam so that every child gets to take a jar home.

STRAWBERRY-ORANGE JAM

equipment:

clean glass canning jars and tops

canning pot (see Resources, page 126)

canning tongs (these are essential for getting hot jars out of the pot)

a funnel for putting the jam into the jars

ingredients:

2 pounds strawberries, hulled and quartered

4 cups vanilla sugar (recipe follows)

3 tablespoons orange juice

zest of 1 orange

To sterilize jars and lids, fill a large canning pot with water, add thoroughly cleaned jam jars and lids, and bring the water to a boil. Boil for 10 minutes. Using canning tongs, remove the sterilized jars from the water and allow to dry and slightly cool on a clean, dry towel.

Meanwhile, to make the jam, gently mash the berries.

In a heavy-bottomed pot over low heat, combine the berries, vanilla sugar, and orange juice and zest. Stir until the sugar has dissolved.

Turn the heat to high and bring the mixture to a boil and cook, stirring, until the mixture reaches 220°F.

Insert the funnel into the first slightly cooled sterilized jar and transfer some of the finished jam into it. Continue with remaining jars and jam. After each jar is filled, add a lid and tighten it in place. Let cool. Store jam in the refrigerator; will keep for 3 weeks.

Makes 5 cups

VANILLA SUGAR

Split 2 vanilla beans in half and scrape the seeds into the jar. Add 4 cups sugar and mix to combine. Bury the vanilla bean pods in the sugar and let sit for 2 weeks, shaking often. Remove beans before using.

Food Fun and Recipes

Strawberry-picking parties are fun and hot! Keep your little pickers happy with a light meal of turkey wraps, dill pickles, and summertime lemonade. If you want to include a taste of what's to come, offer some fresh strawberry jam with your favorite homemade or purchased buttermilk biscuits. Strawberry ice cream (in a cooler, of course) is always a welcome addition with kids!

GINGER-MINT LEMONADE

11¼ cups (90-ounces) homemade or store-bought lemonade

1 (2-inch) piece fresh ginger, peeled and sliced

6 fresh mint leaves (more or less to taste)

Infuse your lemonade with ginger and mint the night before your party. Serve over ice.

Serves 6–8

WHEAT TURKEY WRAPS

4–5 wheat tortillas

½ cup vegan Lemonaise spread (an all-natural citrus mayonnaise available at specialty food stores)

4 slices turkey per tortilla wrap (16–20 slices of turkey)

2 slices havarti cheese per tortilla wrap (8–10 slices of cheese)

baby (or grape) tomatoes, cut in half (about 20 tomatoes)

fresh sprouts or arugula

Place wheat tortillas on a flat surface and spread the Lemonaise over the the top surface of each. Place 4 slices of turkey on each tortilla, covering the whole surface. Layer 2 slices of cheese on the left side of each tortilla and add a few tomato halves on top of the cheese. Place a small handful of sprouts or arugula on top of the tomatoes.

Roll up each tortilla and slice in half. Secure each half by covering the bottom part of the wrap with parchment paper and tying a scrap of the ribbon (leftover from basket decoration) around the top half.

Serves 8–10

Plentiful Autumn

Welcome to Autumn! Autumn is the time of transition, when leaves turn from lush green to hues of burnt reds and golden oranges and yellows. The crisp air invites the wearing of knitted sweaters and handmade scarves. The autumn winds usher in a reflective time, bountiful harvests, and a desire to live in gratitude and awareness. The autumn equinox lands on or near September 22nd and is again when night and day are equal. Autumn is often a time to spend with family close by, sipping cider, eating the last of the corn on the cob straight from the garden, and enjoying the bounty of goodness in our lives. So put your boots on and gather under twinkle tents, tepees, and around your home for some natural fun that your kids will be talking about for many seasons to come!

The pleasure of *Autumn* is...
roasted **pumpkin** seeds; **leaf** stomping;
warm apple cider and *gingerbread* cookies;
abundant garden **squashes** ready to be harvested and made
into soup; a time to say thank-you to all those we love and for
what the *earth* has provided us . . .

Gratitude Birthday Party

You're Invited...

to spend the afternoon honoring a friend's birthday and engaging in a gratitude treasure hunt. The birthday girl or boy creates a list of all the things she/he is grateful for, then hides treasures that represent each of those things for guests to hunt for. Afterward, enjoy warm soup out of a pumpkin bowl, ginger-spiced cookies, and mac-n-cheese.

The Inspiration

This party was inspired by my daughter's birthday, when we started to talk with her about how grateful we were to have her in our lives. When she chimed in with a list of what she was grateful for, we decided to make a list: love, nature, magic, ocean, candy, faeries, art, playing, sweet smells, and friends. This party is also in the autumn, a traditional time to mark the abundance in our lives and tell others how much they mean to us.

PROJECTS AND MATERIALS

Printed invitations
- cardstock paper
- computer and color printer
- string or ribbon (autumn color preferable)

Twinkle tent and outside decor
- recycled tin cans
- fresh autumn flowers or herbs
- silk ribbon
- drill gun
- twinkle lights
- treasure hunt goodies and baskets to hold them

Table decor
- autumn-colored linens
- hollowed-out mini or small pumpkins (to use as soup bowls)
- wooden spoons, forks, and plates
- autumn-colored vases and flowers
- baskets of small apples
- borrowed, thrifted, or handmade cloth napkins

Gratitude banner
- watercolor paper
- watercolor paint and brushes
- hole punch
- marker pen
- silk ribbon

Gratitude friendship flags
- alphabet and other fun stamps and ink pads
- muslin fabric
- twigs collected from fallen branches
- silk ribbon
- sewing machine or hot glue gun and glue sticks

Smile booth
- garden lattice
- fresh greens, herbs, and flowers
- notecards
- alphabet stamps or markers
- hemp string or twine
- wooden letters that spell out "smile booth"
- paints in autumn colors
- hot glue gun

Treasure hunt
- printed cards listed treasures
- small treasures representing each thing on the list
- small baskets to give the children to collect their goodies (you can ask them each to bring one to the party or get a few from a thrift store)

Recipes
- Roasted Veggie Soup
- Mac-n-Cheese
- Ginger-Spiced Acorn Cookies

TIMELINE

3–4 weeks prior to event:
- choose location
- create and deliver invitations
- make gratitude banner
- choose and gather treasure hunt items

1–2 weeks prior to event:
- gather table decor including dishware
- make the gratitude friendship flags

Day prior to event:
- make cookies
- prep veggies for veggie soup
- make mac-n-cheese
- bake cakes, if serving (but don't finish until day of party)
- create the twinkle tent and hang lights

Day of event:
- prepare pumpkin bowls
- set up food table
- set up smile booth
- hide treasures
- hang gratitude banner and friendship flags in trees
- assemble cake
- make soup
- reheat mac-n-cheese

Create Invitations

- Using a computer word processing program, create an invitation in autumn colors that explains the party and its theme, and offers time and place details of the event. Print these on cardstock.

- Create a separate document with information about the gratitude treasure hunt. (See complete explanation on page 76.) This takes some preplanning — you'll need to know in advance where you plan to hide the various treasures in order to write clues about their locations. Print these on cardstock.

- Tie the printed cards together with silk ribbon or string (preferably in a autumn color) and hand-deliver to each guest.

Make Friendship Gratitude Flags and Gratitude Banner

To make friendship gratitude flags:

- Cut 10 X 10-inch pieces of muslin (one for each child coming to the party).

- Fold over one edge about 2 inches and stitch across, leaving a pocket wide enough to slide a stick through. (If you do not have a sewing machine, hand-stitch or use hot glue to make the fold-over pocket.) Slide a stick through the fold-over pocket and tie each end with a ribbon so it can be hung like a banner.

- Stamp each flag with a different child's name. Ask your child what is special about each of the friends coming to his or her party and stamp those notions on that friend's flag. Don't forget to make a special flag for your own child, telling them how they are special to you. Hang the finished flags from the trees at the party so each child attending can find his or her friendship flag.

To make gratitude banner:

- Have your child paint sheets of watercolor paper in a autumn color. When the paint is completely dry, cut the painted paper into 9 (approximately 4 x 6-inch) pieces.

- Write the word "gratitude" — one letter per card — on the cards. Use a hole punch to make two holes on top of each card, and then string the full word together with a silk ribbon. Hang the sign between two trees.

Set the Scene

Locate a **park or use your own backyard** to host this party. Make sure there is enough room to hide the small treasures and for the children to run around.

Hang the friendship gratitude flags and the gratitude banner from tree branches around the party setting.

Create a low-to-the-ground table and **set the table beautifully** with autumn-colored linens, hollowed-out mini or small pumpkins for soup bowls, real linen napkins, wooden plates, forks and spoons, ceramic mugs, autumn-colored flower arrangements, and baskets of small apples for centerpieces. Handmade place cards add a fancy touch to this autumn celebration. If this is being held as a birthday party, create a special circle around the birthday child's place setting with greens and flowers.

Make a **twinkle tent** by hanging twinkle lights from tree to tree. Fashion hanging flower vases out of tin cans by drilling a hole on either side of the top edge of the can. String a piece of silk ribbon through the holes and tie a knot to form a large loop from which to hang the cans. Place fresh flowers or herbs from your garden in the tin cans and hang them from branches near the twinkle lights. It's lovely if you can have your table set up under the twinkle lights.

Assemble a smile booth by decorating a section of lattice with greens, herbs, and flowers from around the garden. Tie them in place with pieces of hemp. Then tie little notecards decorated with each invitee's name. Spell out the words "smile booth" with painted wooden letters and glue them onto the lattice. This creates the perfect spot for each guest to take pictures — formal or silly — with each other.

Gratitude Treasure Hunt

Have each child either bring his or her own small basket or hand them out at the party. Make sure each child has the list of clues to be able to find the treasures. (If you are including the list of clues with the invitations, it is wise to have extra copies printed out for the party in case children forget to bring theirs along.) You may need to have a couple of adults help with this treasure hunt, especially if the children are especially young and cannot yet read.

Ask your child what her very favorite things are. What are the things that make her happy? A child's answers to those questions will likely include a variety of things that include people, ideas, and material objects.

Once you've compiled a list of "favorite things," you will need to relate those things to small physical items that can be hidden for the treasure hunt. For example, if a favorite thing is "love," you could hide small decoupaged hearts (one for each guest); for "nature," you could choose (de-thorned) long stem roses or other garden flowers tied with satin ribbons: for "ocean" we hid seashells; for "candy" we made homemade salted caramels; for "playing" we selected jump ropes; for "sweet smells" we made little bottles of rose and lavender water; and for "friends" we used the friendship gratitude flags. Be creative with the items you select to represent all of your child's "favorite things."

For each "favorite thing" on the list, write a short poem or line that gives clues to where the children can find the goodies that corresponded to each thing. All of this takes time, so give yourself plenty of planning time for this portion of the party. Planning well ahead here will also allow more time to collect items from nature, hand-make goodies, or locate what you need in thrift stores.

Food Fun and Recipe

A autumn party needs food that warms the heart and soul, especially a party that is abundant in warm feelings. I suggest the following recipes for a nice soup, hearty mac-n-cheese, and spiced cookies. Encourage the children to gather their pumpkin bowls filled with roasted veggie soup and sit under the twinkle tent for a autumn feast that won't soon be forgotten.

If you are making this into a birthday party, try making a cake similar to the one on page 72: Make your child's favorite birthday cake in three small cake pans (5 inches across, 2 inches deep). Follow cupcake directions for baking temperature and time. Once baked and cooled, cover each layer's top with a thick covering of whipped cream frosting and stack the layers. Decorate the top layer, add candles, and serve.

ROASTED VEGGIE SOUP

2 zucchini, chopped

4 tomatoes, chopped

3 carrots, chopped

sea salt and pepper to taste

2 tablespoons olive oil

1 tablespoon unsalted butter

2 yellow onions, chopped

3 garlic cloves, chopped

1 tablespoon chopped fresh tarragon

2 (32-ounce) containers vegetable stock

2 vegetable boullion cubes
  (about 2 tablespoons total)

5 cups water

3 stalks celery, chopped

Preheat oven to 250°F.

On a parchment-lined roasting pan, place chopped zucchini, tomatoes, and carrots. Sprinkle lightly with sea salt, pepper, and olive oil. Roast for 40 minutes.

Meanwhile, in a soup pot, melt the butter and add onions, garlic, and tarragon. Sauté for about 6 minutes over low-medium heat. Add the vegetable stock, bouillon cubes, and water; increase heat and bring to a boil.

Add roasted zucchini, tomatoes, and carrots, and the chopped celery to the soup pot. Season with sea salt and pepper to taste, and simmer soup on low for approximately 15 minutes until the flavors are well combined.

Ladle into festive pumpkin bowls and serve immediately.

Serves 10–15

Hearty Mac-n-Cheese

salt

2½ cups elbow macaroni

2 pats unsalted butter, plus extra for greasing

¼ cup all-purpose flour

¾ teaspoon cayenne pepper

½ teaspoon ground nutmeg

½ teaspoon flaxseed powder

1 teaspoon low-sodium soy sauce

2 cups whole milk

1½ cups grated sharp cheddar cheese

1½ cups grated mild white cheddar cheese

½ cup grated Parmesan cheese

½ cup panko breadcrumbs

4 slices country bread, cubed

Preheat oven to 350°F.

Bring a large pot of salted water to a boil, and cook macaroni according to package directions or until al dente. Drain well and set aside.

Meanwhile, prepare a deep ceramic baking dish by buttering the bottom and sides.

Melt 2 pats butter in a large, heavy saucepan over a medium-high heat. Stir in the flour, cayenne, nutmeg, flaxseed powder, and soy sauce. Cook for 1–2 minutes.

Gradually whisk in the milk, continually stirring. Bring white sauce to a boil and then reduce to simmer for about 4–5 minutes, stirring all the time, until the sauce thickens.

Whisk all three types of cheese into the sauce and stir until melted. Season generously with sea salt and pepper.

Stir the cooked pasta through the sauce and remove from the heat.

Spoon the coated pasta into the baking dish and sprinkle the breadcrumbs and bread cubes evenly over the top. Bake for 30 minutes until golden and bubbling.

Serves 15

GINGER-SPICED COOKIES

Try to find a cookie cutter in the shape of an acorn, leaf, or another autumn-related shape.

2 cups all-purpose flour

1 teaspoon baking powder

½ teaspoon baking soda

½ teaspoon sea salt

½ teaspoon freshly grated nutmeg

1 teaspoon ground cinnamon

¼ teaspoon ground ginger

¼ teaspoon ground allspice

2 teaspoons vanilla extract

2 tablespoons molasses

½ cup raw agave nectar

1 cup brown sugar

2 eggs

¼ cup coconut oil

Preheat oven to 350°F. Line cookie sheets with parchment paper and set aside.

In a large mixing bowl, blend together the flour, baking powder, baking soda, salt, nutmeg, cinnamon, ginger, and allspice.

In a separate bowl, combine the vanilla, molasses, agave, and brown sugar, and mix well. Add the eggs, one at a time, then the oil, and blend together until smooth.

Slowly add flour mixture until you create a workable dough. Roll dough out on a floured surface until the dough is about 1/4 thick. Using a cookie cutter, cut cookies shapes from the dough. Once you've cut as many cookies as possible from the rolled-out dough, combine the dough scraps into a ball, reroll, and continue the process until you've used all the dough.

Place cookies on prepared cookie sheets and bake for approximately 15 minutes, until light golden brown, so they will be chewy on the inside. Let cool then store in an airtight container.

Makes 20–25 cookies

Wild Girls Tepee Party

You're Invited...

to leave your manners at the door because this is no fancy tea party. This party is all about running wild, making noise, playing instruments, singing songs, eating delicious tea cake with one hand and roasted corn with the other! This is a party that encourages the wild side of little girls.

The Inspiration

We all know that little girls can be just as rough-and-tumble as their male counterparts. Let them enjoy a "wild" afternoon with feathers in their hair, delicious food, tic-tac-toe games with a homemade stick board, and unrestrained music, all while getting dirty and exploring nature.

PROJECTS AND MATERIALS

Feather stick invitations
- thick natural sticks (one for each girl invited), about 12 inches long
- strips of fabric
- computer and color printer
- feathers
- watercolor paper, paints, and paintbrushes
- mini wooden clothes pins

Tepee tent and outside decor
- canvas tepee, outside tree house, or tent (for a makeshift tepee)
- fresh autumn wildflowers
- torn strips of autumn-colored fabric
- feathers
- hemp rope or twine
- hot glue gun and glue sticks
- recycled bottles
- chalkboard or old piece of wood you can write on with chalk
- chalk
- dream catcher
- simple musical instruments (tambourines, drums, shakers, etc. — have each friend bring some to share)
- baskets with handles

Table decor
- blanket or sheet (on the ground of the tepee or tree house)
- cast-iron pot (for serving corn on the cob)
- old pie tins for plates and vintage forks
- canning jars (for drinking glasses)
- wooden bowls
- tin buckets with ice and mint

Dress-up
- felt pieces in autumn colors
- feathers
- turquoise-colored and wooden beads
- hot glue gun and glue sticks
- Velcro

Twig Tic-Tac-Toe
- 8 10-inch-long sticks
- 20 3-inch-long sticks
- 10 stones
- hot glue gun and glue sticks

Recipes
- Roasted Corn on the Cob
- Veggie Chips
- Herbal Tea Spice Cakes

TIMELINE

2 weeks prior to event:
- choose location such as a park or y our own backyard
- create and deliver invitations
- make hanging fabric banner
- make feathered armbands

I week prior to event:
- gather table decor, dishware
- gather baskets and decorate for wildflower collecting
- gather remaining decor items
- make Twig Tic-Tac-Toe games (2 of them)

Day prior to event:
- make Veggie Chips
- make Herbal Tea Cakes

Day of event:
- set up tepee, tree house, or makeshift tepee tent
- set up hanging decor
- set out instruments and dress-up items
- make roasted corn

Create Invitations

• Have your child watercolor paper in autumn colors. This paper will go through your printer, so choose paper size and thickness accordingly. Set painted papers aside to dry.

• Prepare the invitations using a computer word processing program. Use various fonts in different weights and sizes, and include all the details of your party. Arrange the information on only a portion of the page; you will reduce the page size after printing.

• Feed the painted watercolor paper through a color printer and print out the invitations.

• Cut around the edges of the invitations to make them smaller and create rounded corners.

• Gather 12-inch sticks, one for each girl invited. Hot glue feathers to the top of each stick and tie pieces of torn fabric around the base of the feathers where they make contact with the stick. Attach the invitation to fabric strip with a mini clothespin.

• Deliver these very special invitations to each guest.

Make Feathered Armbands and Headbands

materials and equipment:

strips of felt in autumn colors, 10–12 inches long for armbands, about 18 inches long for headbands, all 1½–2 inches wide

hot glue gun and hot glue

feathers

turquoise-colored and wooden beads

Velcro

Hot glue a small number of feathers and beads to each headband and armband. Glue a 1-inch piece of Velcro to the ends of each band. Let girls use these for dress-up and to take home as a memory of their wild afternoon.

Set the Scene

Host this party in a **park or your own backyard**. Make sure there is room for the girls to **run wild!** Set up your **tepee** or makeshift tepee in a small clearing or open space.

Hang various natural and colorful elements along a long piece of hemp or twine to make decorations that blow on the breeze. Wrap hemp or twine around the necks of recycled bottles, tie securely, fill with **wildflowers**, and hang from a rope. Hot glue feathers to approximately 10-inch-long pieces of hemp and tie those onto the main rope. Tie lengths of torn recycled fabric to the main rope. You can create one or many of these **hanging decorations**, depending on your setup and space. Also hang a dream catcher (if you have one) from the inside or edge of the tepee or tree house.

Create a **wild girls picnic area** by using sheets, blankets, and pieces of wood to create a simple rustic setting. Use a large cast-iron pot to hold roasted corn, wooden bowls for veggie chips and herbal teacakes, and old tin pie plates and jars for eating and drinking. Rustic, natural, and simple — nothing formal here!

Fill **tin buckets with ice and mint leaves**. This is a wonderful refresher for wild girls on the go. Prepare a small space with instruments to encourage the girls to **make music**. Decorate the handles of **baskets** with torn strips of recycled fabric and have these available for collecting wildflowers and other natural elements.

Play Twig Tic-Tac-Toe

Prepare two game setups:

- Collect eight 10-inch-long sticks and twenty 3-inch-long sticks.

- Make the "board" by using a hot glue gun to glue the longer sticks together — two sticks going down and two going across at right angles for each "board".

- Make the "X" pieces by using a hot glue gun to glue the shorter sticks into 10 X-shaped pieces (five per game).

- Gather 10 smooth stones to use as the "O" pieces (five per game).

- Place the "board" on any surface you want and play classic tic-tac-toe.

Food Fun and Recipes

This tepee party is for wild girls only! The food must be easy to eat and no one can be fussy about the mess. Girls will love to munch on roasted corn, veggie chips, and herbal teacakes. Quench their thirst with some simple lemony iced tea.

ROASTED CORN ON THE COB

8 ears fresh corn, husks pulled back and tied with twine, silks removed

butter

salt and pepper to taste

1 tablespoon chopped fresh thyme

Preheat the oven to 350°F.

Lay out 8 pieces of foil, each large enough to wrap a single ear of corn. Place one ear on each piece of foil, rub each one with butter, and then season with salt and pepper and thyme.

Wrap each ear tightly in its foil, then roast in the oven for 20 minutes.

Loosen (but don't remove) foil wrappers to release some heat, and serve warm.

Serves 8

Veggie Chips

2 sweet potatoes, peeled

2 beets, peeled

2 carrots, peeled

2 yellow potatoes

olive oil for coating

salt and pepper to taste

Preheat oven to 375°F. Line two baking sheets with parchment paper.

Use a mandoline slicer to cut the sweet potatoes, beets, carrots, and yellow potatoes into very thin slices.

Put all vegetable slices in a large bowl, drizzle with olive oil, and season to taste with salt and pepper.

Spread seasoned vegetable slices in a single layer over both prepared baking sheets. Bake for 18 minutes.

Remove from oven and let veggies cool completely on baking sheets. Combine in a large serving bowl and serve at room temperature.

Serves 4–5

HERBAL TEA SPICE CAKES

This recipe requires a large heart-shaped cookie cutter.

2 cups all-purpose flour

1½ teaspoon baking powder

½ teaspoon baking soda

¼ teaspoon ground cloves

¼ teaspoon ground nutmeg

1 teaspoon ground cinnamon

¼ teaspoon ground ginger

½ cup cocoa powder

4 tablespoons (½ stick) butter

1 cup brown sugar

½ cup raw agave nectar

½ cup prepared orange spice herbal tea, cooled to room temperature

½ teaspoon vanilla extract

¼ cup coconut oil (or vegetable oil)

2 eggs

1 cup heavy cream

confectioners' sugar for sprinkling

fresh fruit (as garnish)

Preheat oven to 350°F. Grease and lightly flour two 8 x 11-inch cake pans. Set aside.

In a large mixing bowl, mix together flour, baking powder, baking soda, cloves, nutmeg, cinnamon, ginger, and cocoa powder. Set aside.

In the mixing bowl of an electric mixer set on medium speed, beat the butter and brown sugar together for about 30 seconds. Add the agave, tea, and vanilla, and beat until well mixed.

Add the oil. Then add the eggs one at a time, beating after adding each egg.

Add the dry ingredients and the cream alternately into the egg and butter mixture, beating on low speed after each addition, just until combined.

Divide batter into prepared cake pans. Bake for 35–40 minutes or until toothpick inserted into the center of the cake comes out clean. Cool cakes in pans on wire rack.

When cakes are completely cooled, remove from pans and place on a cutting board. Use a large heart-shaped cookie cutter to cut as many heart shapes as you can from the finished cakes. Sprinkle the tops of each heart cakelet with confectioners' sugar and serve with your choice of fruit.

Serves 8–10

Upcycle Art Party

You're Invited...

to reuse, recycle, and upcycle old things into fabulous new art! Recycled rainbow crayons and upcycled wool sweater dream pillows are the crafts of the day, and there will be no shortage of fun as these projects take form. Snack on Grilled Cheese with Apple Butter, Thyme Potato Chips, and a special recipe for Pumpkin Harvest Tea Bread.

The Inspiration

Children love making art, and using recycled materials helps them feel like they are doing something sustainable for our planet. Almost every family has a box of broken crayons and an outgrown or un-wearable wool sweater to spare, so why not use them as the basics for fun art projects? This is a super fun party with a very eco-friendly twist.

PROJECTS AND MATERIALS

Paintbrush invitations
- paintbrushes (1 for each child invited)
- alphabet stamps and stamp pad
- a fine-point pen or a computer and printer
- vintage or recycled Kraft paper tags

Table decor
- brown kraft paper (large sheet to cover table)
- art supplies in recycled glass jars (color pencils, paints, and paintbrushes, etc.)

Dream pillows
- recycled sweater
- dried herbs (chamomile, lavender, and calendula), rice, or seeds
- muslin or other lightweight cotton fabric
- needle and thread or sewing machine
- fabric shears
- embroidery thread
- ruler

Recycled rainbow crayons
- broken crayons, wrappers removed
- muffin tins or other tin molds
- vegetable spray
- oven
- cooling rack

Recipes
- Grilled Cheese with Apple Butter
- Thyme Potato Chips
- Pumpkin Harvest Tea Bread

TIMELINE

2 weeks to 1 month prior to event:
- choose your location
- create and deliver invitations

1 week prior to event:
- gather all table decor
- gather all art supplies
- make inserts for dream pillows

Day prior to event:
- organize supplies by activity
- make Pumpkin Harvest Tea Bread
- make Apple Butter

Day of event:
- decorate space and table
- set up craft stations or work areas
- set up a panini press, griddle, or outdoor grill with a grill press; make grilled cheese sandwiches
- cook potato chips

Create Invitations

- Stamp the word "ART" on the top of vintage or recycled kraft paper tags (4–5 inches long, 2–3 inches wide works best); one per invitation.

- Write out the invitation details on the tags. If you want your guests to bring some of the recycled items to the party, be sure to include those details on the invitation. The information can be handwritten or typed depending on your preference.

- Tie each tag to a paintbrush.

- Hand-deliver invitations to each guest. Asking that each child bring his or her invitation paintbrush to the party will ensure plenty of paintbrushes to go around.

Set the Scene

Children love to **create in nature**, and on a lovely autumn day, this party would be perfect outside. However, if the weather just isn't cooperating, the same decor can be brought inside for a warm and fun atmosphere.

Cover a table with a **kraft paper tablecloth**. Fill recycled glass jars with various **art supplies** — color pencils, paints, paintbrushes, crayons, markers, etc., and scatter them over the table so kids can reach at least a few things. Invite your guests to get their **creative juices flowing** right from the beginning of the party. (If this paper tablecloth gets too wet from paints before the food is served, you may want to replace it with a fresh one and remove any liquid art supplies for the second round. The original "tablecloth" can be hung up as a mural.)

Create a **sewing station** and a **crayon station** for each child to cycle through. Displaying all necessary art supplies at each station will make for a lovely, colorful presentation with no extras necessary.

The goal here is to use what you have, or find things in thrift stores to upcycle into new treasures. Kids will have fun locating the items to upcycle, so be sure to include them in the search for craft items. See how close to zero waste you can get with your party, and discuss the reasons why such a goal is important to your children. Everything that is used should be able to be **reused, recycled, or composted**.

Make Recycled Rainbow Crayons

Be sure to have extra paper ready, because kids won't be able to resist trying out these awesome rainbow crayons just as soon as they're made.

• Preheat the oven to 150°F.

• Set up a crayon station by placing big bowls out for each child to deposit their broken and old crayons (wrappers removed) into upon arriving to the party.

• Spray the muffin tin or individual tins with vegetable spray; wipe out any excess oil.

• Have each child pick 3 to 5 crayons from the bowl, and break them into small bits. Place them into one of the muffin cups, or into an individual tin. If using individual tins, place them onto a baking sheet.

• Bake the crayons for 45 minutes, or until fully melted. Pop them out and allow to cool completely on a wire rack.

Make Upcycled Wool Sweater Dream Pillow

We found that this project works best if an adult does a little prep work (including making the pillow inserts, cutting the pillow sides from the sweater, and threading needles that the children will sew with) in advance of the project. Once the setup is complete, have the children sit in a circle while an adult demonstrates a simple blanket stitch. As the kids get going on their own pillows, you are then free to move among the children and help where needed.

- Before the party begins, make the pillow inserts. Each insert requires two 4 × 4-inch squares of muslin or other lightweight cotton fabric. Using a 1/4-inch seam allowance, sew around the square (with right sides together), leaving a 3-inch opening in one side. Turn the fabric right-side out; fill with dried herbs (such as lavender, chamomile, or calendula), rice, flax, etc. of your choice; and hand-sew the opening closed. Have a pillow insert ready for each dream pillow to be made at the party.

- Have a felted wool sweater for each child, or alternatively, have each child bring a pre-felted old wool sweater to the party. (For instructions on felting a wool sweater, see page 120.)

- For each pillow, cut two 5 × 5-inch squares from the felted fabric.

- Thread needles with embroidery thread, and have each child sew a blanket stitch around three sides of his or her square. Place the dream pillow insert inside the sweater cover, and have the children sew up the fourth side.

Food Fun and Recipes

For this project-filled art party, have some easy-to-eat snack foods readily available for the children. Their little hands will be busy all day, so feed their tummies well!

GRILLED CHEESE WITH APPLE BUTTER

This recipe uses a slow-cooker (for the apple butter) and a panini press, griddle, or outdoor grill to grill the sandwiches. The apple butter takes several hours to cook, so be sure to make it at least a day before the party. The recipe makes 1½ cups of apple butter; the sandwich recipe instructions are for one sandwich. Allow a half to a whole sandwich per child.

apple butter:

8 Granny Smith or other tart apples, cored, peeled, and sliced
1 cup dried-sweetened, cranberries
¼ cup packed brown sugar
1 teaspoon ground cinnamon
¾ teaspoon ground nutmeg
1 cup plus 1 teaspoon water
1 teaspoon cornstarch

apple butter: Combine the apple slices, cranberries, sugar, cinnamon, nutmeg, and 1 cup water in a slow-cooker and stir to combine. Cook on low, covered, for 5 hours.

Whisk 1 teaspoon water and cornstarch together in a bowl. Add to the apple butter in the slow-cooker and continue to cook on low for 1 hour more.

Use a potato masher or a hand-blender to mix or mash the fully cooked apple butter until it is the desired consistency. Chill in the refrigerator before serving.

grilled cheese:

2 slices rustic whole wheat or special savory bread
  (such as rosemary sourdough or cranberry walnut)
apple butter (see recipe above)
2–4 slices Muenster cheese

grilled cheese: Preheat panini press, griddle, or outdoor grill.

Spread one side of each slice of bread with a thin layer of apple butter. Add cheese slices to one piece of bread and cover with the second slice of bread. Place on panini press or grill and cook until desired darkness.

Make as many sandwiches as you will need to satisfy your guests. Slice into triangles and serve.

Makes 1 sandwich and 1½ cups apple butter

THYME POTATO CHIPS

2 potatoes
oil for frying
kosher salt
2 tablespoons chopped thyme

Using a mandoline, slice potatoes into very thin slices.

Fill a large heavy-bottomed saucepan about a third full with oil and heat until the oil reaches 350°F..

Add the potato slices to the hot oil in small batches and fry until golden brown, about 2 minutes. Drain on paper towels and season with salt and thyme. Serve warm or at room temperature.

Serves 4–6

PUMPKIN HARVEST TEA BREAD

This is a recipe that has been in my family for as long as I can remember, and autumn is never complete without its presence. You can omit the walnuts if desired.

bread:
1¾ cups of all-purpose flour
1 teaspoon baking soda
¼ teaspoon ground ginger
1 teaspoon ground cinnamon
½ teaspoon salt
¼ teaspoon ground cloves
8 tablespoons (1 stick) butter
1 cup sugar
2 eggs

¾ cup pumpkin puree
¾ cup chocolate chips
½ cup chopped walnuts,
 plus 1 tablespoon for sprinkling

glaze:
⅛ cup confectioners' sugar
¼ teaspoon ground nutmeg
⅛ teaspoon ground cinnamon
2 tablespoons heavy cream

Preheat oven to 350°F. Use cooking spray to grease a 5 x 9-inch loaf pan.

In a medium bowl, mix flour, baking soda, ginger, cinnamon, salt, and cloves together and set aside. In the bowl of an electric mixer, cream butter and sugar on medium speed. Add eggs and beat well. Turn the mixer to low speed, and add dry ingredients alternately with pumpkin. Stir in chocolate chips and nuts.

Pour batter into prepared pan, and sprinkle with extra chopped nuts. Bake for 50–60 minutes, until a toothpick inserted into the center of the bread comes out clean.

Make the glaze while the bread is baking. In a medium bowl, blend sugar, nutmeg, cinnamon, and cream together until it forms a nice drizzle topping consistency.

When bread is almost cooled, remove from pan and spoon glaze over the top.

Makes 1 loaf

Enchanting Winter

Welcome to Winter!

The dawning of winter brings with it the longest night of the year, and the promise of the return of more sun. The winter solstice falls on or near December 21, though it is often overlooked in the hustle and bustle of the holiday season. Winter is a time of introspection, for adults and children alike, and it is when we should find ourselves looking inward to discover how we want to blossom when spring arrives. Winter is the perfect season for evenings spent in front of the fire, diving into a great story, and sharing time with friends and family. So gather together to sip comforting soups, eat fresh breads, and enjoy warm drinks that satisfy heart and soul.

The wonder of Winter is…

building snowmen; gathering around a crackling fire; creating play forts made from every pillow in the house; sipping hot chocolate; sweet kisses under the mistletoe; ponds turned over to ice rinks; beautifully wrapped packages hand-delivered to those we love.; the solitude that a heavy snowstorm brings, the twinkle lights that glitter from rooftops; candles lit to usher in the glow of what is to come …

Winter Solstice Party

You're Invited...

to dig out your most comfy sweater, grab a cup of warming chai, and gather around the fireplace for a wintry celebration. This time of year, when the cold air is nipping at your door, is a perfect time to be indoors and invite more quiet into the home. Create salt dough and natural beeswax ornaments, and make beeswax candles. Join around the table for a filling, warming soup and delight in Rosemary-Lemon Cookies and Cranberry Fluff Cake Crumble.

The Inspiration

The winter solstice is the darkest day of the year, making it a welcome day to gather friends for a party around the fire. Children love to create with their hands, making gifts for one another and others, and this party is inspired by those creations. The cold outside is balanced by the warmth of good friends, a spiced chai drink, and hearty soup.

PROJECTS AND MATERIALS

Snowflake invitations
- white and cream decorative cardstock
- paper doily
- computer and printer
- paper paste (such as Mod Podge)

Table decor
- large chalkboard menu
- white ceramic bowls, canning jars with straws, and mugs,
- pine greenery and pinecones
- candles

Beeswax ornaments and candle dipping
- 2 blocks natural beeswax
- plastic chocolate molds or small metal tart molds
- ribbon, jute, twine, or vintage string
- oil spray
- toothpicks
- large glass jar for water
- large recycled metal container (for hot wax)

- 12-inch pieces of thick braided wicks (one per candle)
- double boiler, slow-cooker, or large glass jar (for melting beeswax and will be permanently covered with wax)

Salted dough ornaments
- flour
- salt
- warm water
- watercolor paints and brushes
- glitter

Recipes
- Cheesy Potato Soup with Honeyed Walnuts
- Rosemary-Lemon Cookies
- Cranberry Fluff Cake Crumble
- Warm Chai

TIMELINE

2 weeks to 1 month prior to event:
- create your invitations and deliver them to your guests
- purchase beeswax blocks

1 week prior to event:
- gather all table decor and dishware
- purchase all remaining ingredients for ornament making

Day prior to event:
- make Cheesy Potato Soup
- make lemon cookies
- prepare salted dough and cut out ornaments
- gather all other ingredients for remaining recipes
- decorate your home

Day of event:
- make all remaining recipes
- melt beeswax (begin this well before guests arrive so that it is ready upon their arrival)
- create a kid-friendly workspace with salt dough ornaments and decorating goodies
- set up space for candle dipping process

Create Invitations

- Using a computer word processing program, create an invitation that lists your party details and invites your guests to your event. Print these on cardstock.

- Paint a thin layer of paper paste (such as Mod Podge) on the back center of each card and affix a doily in place. The doily should be large enough to overlap the sides of the card.

- Hand-deliver these elegant winter snowflake invitations to your guests.

Set the Scene

The **winter solstice** is the darkest day of the year, so adding **light and warmth** is essential. Place as many **candles** as possible around your space, preferably using **natural beeswax**, as it has the most inviting smell and enhances the mood of any group.

Light the fire. If you have a **fireplace**, use it! If you are hosting your party outdoors, create a large bonfire to celebrate. (Always check with your local fire department for regulations before outdoor fires.)

Set a table with white ceramic dishes and canning jars with lids with fun straws for a cranberry-orange juice along with mugs for hot chai. Embellish the table with **pine greens**. Consider placing a few whole, raw cranberries and pinecones on the table for color and decoration. Encourage a beautifully decorated sit-down meal. Setting the table, sitting down together, and toasting to the season is a favorite for children of all ages.

Decide before the party begins how each child can participate in **making the ornaments**. We have found that this is a party that is better suited to a small crowd of around 4–5 children. Letting each one have a turn at pouring the beeswax, **making candles**, and creating their ornaments from start to finish takes time, so planning ahead is essential.

Create a workspace where the children can gather to **decorate their salt dough ornaments**. With paint and glitter and other small decorative elements, this can get messy.

Make Beeswax Ornaments and Candles

Please note that beeswax can take an hour or longer to melt slowly. You will need to plan ahead and have this done before the children arrive. Plus, it makes your space smell lovely, and sets the mood for when your guests arrive.

This makes 20 beeswax ornaments if using small tins or plastic chocolate molds. Place 2 blocks of natural beeswax in a large bowl over a pot of boiling water (double boiler method), in a glass canning jar immersed a third of the way in a pot of slowly boiling water (bain-marie method), or in a large slow-cooker.

Important: Beeswax is very difficult to remove from kitchenware and appliances. You can use an inexpensive slow-cooker that you keep just for melting beeswax or a metal bowl that you designate for beeswax purposes only. Don't bother trying to clean it afterwards, as it doesn't come out!

To make beeswax ornaments:

• Lightly spray the molds with cooking oil spray and wipe out any excess.

• Pour melted wax into your molds and allow to partially set. After 5–10 minutes, the consistency will be at the right consistency to place your ribbon or twine directly into the mold. If you prefer, use a toothpick to poke a hole through the top of the ornament for hanging later.

• Once the beeswax has cooled completely (usually takes 1–2 hours), carefully unmold the ornaments and hang. Please note that since your ornaments need time to dry and cool, it is best to do this activity at the beginning of the party.

To make beeswax candles:

• Pour the remaining melted wax into a tall metal container and place another tall jar filled with cold water next to it. You may want to place something underneath your project if you are concerned about wax dripping onto the surface of a table or floor. Because of the hot wax, this activity should be carefully supervised by an adult.

• Give each child his or her 12-inch piece of thick braided wick string (available at art supply stores). Have them dip the string almost all the way into the hot wax, leaving about 3 inches on top, and then immediately dip it into the cold water. Repeat this process until the beeswax candle has formed.

• Set candles aside to dry and give to the children at the end of the party to take home.

Make Salted Dough Ornaments

Because these are baked slowly, it is best to make and bake the ornaments in advance of the party.

2 cups flour
1 cup salt
1 cup warm water
watercolor paints and brushes
glitter

Preheat oven to 200°F. Line a cookie sheet with parchment paper and set aside.

In the bowl of an electric mixer, combine the flour and salt. Add the warm water slowly, and mix until you have a workable dough consistency (not too sticky).

Roll out dough to ¼-inch thickness. Use cookie cutters to cut out shapes from the dough and transfer shapes to the prepared cookie sheet.

Use a thick toothpick or skewer to poke a hole in the top of each ornament. Make sure that the hole goes all the way through the dough. Because the hole will shrink during baking, make sure that it is large enough not to close completely.

Bake for 4–6 hours. Remove and cool completely.

Place the baked, cooled ornaments on a worktable among the watercolor paints and brushes. Let the guests paint their own ornaments. If they want to use glitter, they should sprinkle glitter over the top of the painted ornament when the paint is still wet so it will adhere.

Makes 24 ornaments

Food Fun and Recipes

Keep the food warm and rustic with this potato soup and some sweet-savory lemon herb treats. If you want to add to the meal, the soup goes well with a classic grilled cheese, or simply serve with a crusty hearty bread or cornbread. Serve with warm chai, or make a simple cranberry-orange drink by adding sliced oranges and floating cranberries to a pitcher of cranberry juice. The cranberry cake is a festive dessert in wintertime.

CHEESY POTATO SOUP WITH HONEYED WALNUTS

1 cup chopped walnuts

½ cup honey

2 tablespoons butter

1½ yellow onions, chopped

2 garlic cloves, minced

1 tablespoon minced fresh tarragon

1 tablespoon minced fresh rosemary

½ tablespoon minced fresh thyme

2 pieces celery, chopped

½ cup chopped mushrooms (any variety)

2 pounds potatoes, peeled and chopped

4 cups (32-ounces) chicken or vegetable broth

2 cup water

2 pinches cayenne pepper

salt and pepper to taste

2 cups shredded white cheddar cheese

Preheat oven to 350°F.

On a large rimmed baking sheet lined with parchment paper, arrange a single layer of walnuts and coat with honey. Bake the walnuts for about 15 minutes, and set aside.

Meanwhile, set a large saucepan over medium-high heat and melt butter for 1–2 minutes. Add onion, garlic, tarragon, rosemary, thyme, celery, and mushrooms. Sauté for 5–7 minutes. Add potatoes, broth, and water, and bring to a boil.

Add cayenne and salt and pepper. Cover, turn the heat down to a simmer, and cook for 30 minutes or until potatoes soften.

Puree with a blender and return to a clean pot.

To serve, stir cheese into hot soup until melted and fully incorporated. Add salt and spices to taste, and garnish with honeyed walnuts.

Serves 8

ROSEMARY-LEMON COOKIES

2 cups all-purpose flour

½ teaspoon baking powder

¼ teaspoon baking soda

¼ teaspoon salt

1 tablespoon chopped fresh rosemary

8 tablespoons (1 stick) butter, softened

½ cup raw agave nectar

½ cup pure cane sugar

½ cup freshly squeezed lemon juice

zest of 1 lemon

1 large egg

¼ cup heavy cream

Preheat the oven to 350°F. Line a baking sheet with parchment paper and set aside.

In a large bowl, mix together flour, baking powder, baking soda, salt, and rosemary.

In the bowl of an electric mixer, cream together butter, agave nectar, and sugar. Add lemon juice and zest and mix. Then mix in egg and cream.

Add the flour mixture to the butter mixture about ¼ cup at a time. Once the flour mixture is incorporated, remove the dough from the bowl and knead the dough with your hands until all ingredients are fully combined.

Drop dough in tablespoon-size portions, about 3 inches apart, on the prepared cookie sheet. Press down on each cookie with your thumb to flatten slightly. Bake for 8–10 minutes, until lightly browned on the bottom.

Remove from the oven and transfer cookies to wire racks to cool completely.

Makes 15–20 cookies

CRANBERRY FLUFF CAKE CRUMBLE

This recipe uses a bundt pan.

3 cups fresh or frozen cranberries	10 egg whites
1 cup raw agave nectar	1¼ teaspoons cream of tartar
1½ cups all-purpose flour	1¼ teaspoons vanilla extract
½ cup coconut sugar	¼ teaspoon salt
1 cup pure cane sugar, divided	

In a medium saucepan over medium heat, combine cranberries and agave nectar. Cook for about 5 minutes, until the mixture begins to boil. Reduce heat and let simmer for about 5 minutes, and then remove from heat and set aside to use as a topping.

Preheat the oven to 350°F.

In a large bowl, combine flour, coconut sugar, and pure cane sugar, and set aside.

In the bowl of an electric mixer, beat egg whites, cream of tartar, vanilla, and salt on high speed until foamy.

Gradually add flour-sugar mixture to the egg whites, beating until stiff peaks form.

Gently pour batter into an ungreased 10-inch bundt pan. Bake for 35–40 minutes or until cake springs back when lightly touched and cracks feel dry. Remove from oven and immediately invert pan; cool cake completely before removing from pan.

Cut cake into large pieces, then crumble pieces into individual ramekins or bowls. Top with cranberry topping and serve.

Serves 12

WARM CHAI

The following is my favorite chai recipe — a basic masala recipe that boils everything together for a quick and easy drink that kids will love.

4 whole cloves	⅛ teaspoon black peppercorns, ground
2 cardamom pods, crushed and lightly roasted	2 cups milk
1 cinnamon stick, broken into pieces	2 cups water
1 piece fresh ginger, about the size of a small grape, peeled and chopped	2 tablespoons sugar
	2 tablespoons loose decaffeinated black tea (or 2 tea bags)

Combine the spices with the milk, water, and sugar. Bring to boil. Boil for 10 minutes, add tea, and continue to boil for 2–4 minutes more.

Strain and serve in mugs.

Serves 4–6

Knights and Dragon Quest Party

You're Invited…

to come to this party dressed as a knight. You'll stage a play about knights, a dragon, and a princess. One brave boy will play the part of the dragon and several knights will show off their sword skills and bravery to rescue the maiden! Afterward, everyone's invited to eat, drink, and be merry at a Renaissance feast that includes Shepherd's Pie, Dragon Soup, and Dutch Oven Apple-Berry Cobbler.

The Inspiration

Boys love adventure and when you mix it with a little (pretend) danger, all the better! Gathering boys together creates a lot of energy, so having a party set with a Renaissance theme offers them a natural environment to explore their exuberant creativity.

PROJECTS AND MATERIALS

Burned-edge Renaissance-style invitations
- lined notebook paper
- computer and color printer
- candle (flame used to burn the paper edges)
- twine or hemp

Outdoor stage and decor
- long curtains or pieces of fabric to hang as a stage curtain
- big wooden clips (to hang fabric)
- string of small white lights

Table decor
- enamel dishware, bowls, and mugs
- rustic wooden bowls for extra fresh veggies to share
- burlap (for tablecloth)
- wild herbs and raw carrots (for centerpiece)
- large metal bucket
- wooden spoons and forks

Dress-up
- dragon costume
- shields and wooden swords
- knight costumes (have each boy bring his own)
- a princess or fair maiden costume (if one of the boys has a sister or friend willing to play the part of course!)

Recipes
- Shepherd's Pie
- Dragon Soup
- Dutch Oven Apple-Berry Cobbler

TIMELINE

2 weeks prior to event:
- create and deliver invitations
- gather costumes from thrift stores and make sure guests have what they need

1 week prior to event:
- gather table decor and dishware
- gather stage props (swords, shields, curtains, fabric, and white lights)

Day prior to event:
- make Shepherd's Pie
- make Dragon Soup
- prepare cobbler, but bake the next day

Day of event:
- set up stage area
- set out costumes in either an old trunk or baskets
- set up table and dishwashing station

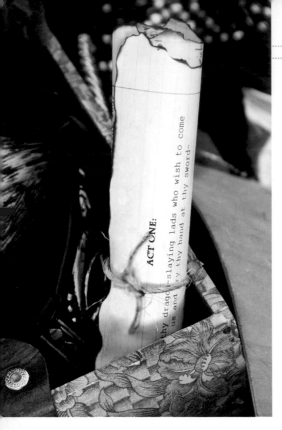

Create Invitations

- Prepare the invitations using a computer word processing program. Arrange the information in the center of the page; you will reduce the page size slightly after printing.

- Feed the lined notebook paper through a color printer and print out the invitations.

- Light a candle and carefully burn the edges of the paper. This step should be done only by an adult and over the kitchen sink or another fireproof area (in case the charred bits of paper fall or the flaming paper is accidentally dropped).

- Roll up the finished invitation and tie with a piece of twine or hemp.

- Have your child wear his knight costume as he delivers the invitations to each guest.

Set the Scene

If you live in a region that is still relatively warm in the early winter months, you can host this party outside. Whether **indoors or out**, you may be lucky enough to find an existing and available stage where you can host this party. However, don't despair if you need to create a stage in the park or your yard, or within your house or another indoor space.

Hang old curtains or pieces of long fabric to make your space look like a stage. If you have an existing stage to work with, this part of setup is easy. If not, and you're outside, simply hang a rope from tree to tree, hang long pieces of cloth over it, and clip it into place with large wooden clips. Indoor stages can be created by curtaining off a wide doorframe or a corner of a room. **Hang white lights** along the rope to make the stage area look more formal and special.

If you are considering this party, chances are you have at least one **knight costume** or perhaps a **dragon costume** in your dress-up stash. If you have neither or if you don't have them in abundance (enough to outfit your entire guest list), you can ask the party attendees to bring their own costumes. Don't forget to check out your local thrift store for possible knight- and dragon-related gear. It's also pretty easy to concoct makeshift knight costumes using old clothes. If you do not have swords, use long sticks found in nature and paint them silver, leaving about 4 inches unpainted at the bottom to use for the handle. Wrap the handle with a piece of brown fake leather.

Set out an old trunk or large baskets with the costumes. (If you are borrowing costumes or guests are bringing costumes to share, you may want to make sure every costume has a name on an inside label so there are no mix-ups when sorting them out later.

Hopefully you will have one or two sisters attending the party who will be willing to play the part of the fair maiden/princess. They should attend dressed for the part.

Create a **rustic table** using **burlap for a tablecloth** and enamel plates or old pie tins for plates. Have a large metal bucket filled with water and another large bucket for scraps of composting food, so the boys can rinse their own dishes as they would have had to do in the **Renaissance period**. Use enamel mugs for the dessert and wooden spoons and forks. Decorate the center of the table with bowls of raw carrots and sprigs of herbs and twigs.

The Play + Quest

Before any action commences, make sure to set some ground rules around the sword play: No hitting each other with swords or sticks. They are props for play and should not to be used to hurt anyone.

Begin by letting each boy choose a costume (unless your guests arrived already dressed for their roles) and allowing everyone to get dressed. Invite one (or two, if you have enough costumes) boys to play dragons. Don't forget to outfit a princess.

Give each boy the knightly task of coming up with a plan to save the maiden from the dragon's cave. They may surprise you with how creative they can get, but if they do need some help organizing their play, here is a basic outline to get them started:

Act I: As the princess sleeps, a dragon comes to her bedside and captures her. [Princess and dragon exit stage and hide.]

The knights enter, discover the princess missing and some suspicious-looking dragon tracks, and make a plan to save her.

Act II: The knights prepare for their quest to save the princess by gathering supplies — swords, shields, food, water, etc. The group of knights begins the quest.

Act III: The knights arrive at the dragon's cave, but don't see the princess. They think the dragon has eaten the princess, so they challenge the dragon to a duel.

The dragon refuses the challenge and explains that he didn't eat the princess — she escaped. [Dragon is sad; knights are surprised.]

Act IV: The princess returns to the scene and asks the dragon why he captured her in the first place. He explains that he just wanted someone to play with.

The knights, in an act true to their code of chivalry, invite the dragon and the princess back to the castle for some play time and a feast! [This is a fun time to serve the food and let all the characters, real and imagined, enjoy the real party feast.]

The knights, dragon, and princess exit the stage happily. [Then return for plenty of bows, of course.]

The end.

The party host or the kids involved may want to come up with different scenes that give each guest a special quest or a chance to shine. With knights, dragons, a princess, or some treasures involved, the possibilities are endless.

Food Fun and Recipes

To stay in theme with this party, go Renaissance! Keep it fun by creating a sign that says Eat, Drink, and Be Merry Here, and place it by the food. Try using your best English accent when telling the boys what is on the menu and watch their faces light up when you say Dragon Soup, Shepherd's Pie, and Apple-Berry Cobbler! Let them clank their mugs on the table when they want more. (No, this behavior isn't considered polite today, but it does feel authentic to the boys.) Most fun for the chef will be when the boys all give shouts of "huzzah, huzzah" to thank the chef for her food!

DRAGON SOUP

2 tablespoons butter

2 yellow onions, chopped

2 garlic cloves, minced

1 tablespoon minced fresh tarragon

1 tablespoon minced fresh rosemary

½ tablespoon minced fresh thyme

4 cups (32 ounces) chicken or vegetable broth

2 chicken or vegetable bouillon cubes

2 cups water

1 tablespoon Bragg Liquid Aminos or low-sodium soy sauce

4 stalks celery, chopped

4 carrots, chopped

4 zucchini, chopped

2 pinches cayenne pepper

salt and pepper to taste

In a large saucepan over medium-high heat, heat the butter for 1–2 minutes. Add the onion, garlic, tarragon, rosemary, and thyme. Sauté for 5–7 minutes.

Add broth, bouillon cubes, water, and Bragg's or soy sauce. Increase heat and bring to a boil. Once boiling, turn down the heat to medium, and add the celery, carrots, and zucchini. Add the cayenne and salt and pepper to taste. Cover, turn the heat down to low, and simmer the soup for 15 minutes or until the zucchini soften.

Serve warm with rustic bread . . . Pass the butter.

Serves 10–12

SHEPHERD'S PIE

This recipe is simple to make in individual pie pans. It requires 6 individual (6-inch) foil pie pans.

1 tablespoon olive oil

2 tablespoons Bragg Liquid Aminos or low-sodium soy sauce

2 yellow onions, chopped small

3 carrots, chopped small

3 stalks celery, chopped small

1 cup frozen peas

1 tablespoon chopped fresh rosemary

2 garlic cloves, minced

1 tablespoon all-purpose flour

4 cups (32 ounces) chicken broth

2 pinches cayenne pepper

salt and pepper to taste

4–5 cups mashed potatoes

1 cup panko breadcrumbs

In a large saucepan over medium-high heat, heat olive oil. Stir in the Bragg's or soy sauce. Add the onions, carrots, celery, peas, rosemary, and garlic. Sauté for 5–7 minutes.

Add flour and mix thoroughly. Add broth, cayenne, and salt and pepper, and bring to a boil. Once it reaches a boil, remove the saucepan from the heat and set aside.

Preheat the oven to broil.

Scoop some of the broth mixture, making sure to get a little broth and mostly veggies, into each individual pie pan. Top each with a scoop of mashed potatoes and sprinkle breadcrumbs on top.

Place the pie pans on a baking sheet and put under the broiler for 3–4 minutes or until browned on top.

Serve warm.

Makes 6 small pies

DUTCH OVEN APPLE-BERRY COBBLER

This recipe requires a Dutch oven. Prepare it in advance and bake just prior to serving.

8 Gala apples, chopped

½ tablespoon ground nutmeg

½ tablespoon ground cinnamon

½ tablespoon ground allspice

1 teaspoon salt

2 cups blackberries, blueberries, or any fresh berries

juice of 1 lemon

3 cups quick oats

2 cups brown sugar

½ cup diced dates

1 teaspoon baking powder

8 tablespoons unsalted butter (1 stick), softened

Preheat oven to 350°F.

In a large bowl, mix the apples with nutmeg, cinnamon, allspice, and salt. Add the berries and lemon juice, and mix together with your hands.

In a separate large bowl, mix oats, sugar, dates, baking powder, and butter together to form a loose dough or crumble.

Press most of the dough into the bottom of a Dutch oven to form a nice base, reserving some to crumble on the top. Pour the apple and berry mixture over the crust, and top with the remaining crumble mixture.

Bake, covered, for 40–45 minutes until nicely browned. Serve warm, directly from the Dutch oven. You may want to top with vanilla bean ice cream.

Serves 8–10

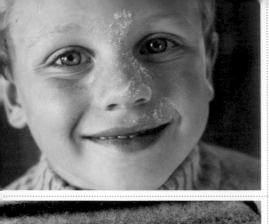

Community Cooking Party

You're Invited...

to don a special upcycled sweater apron and gather to bake for the holidays. Baking for others during the winter season brings together communities and warms the heart and tummy! Make Chocolate-Orange Bread and Carrot-Apple Muffins, wrap the treats in lovely packages topped with watercolor blessings, then head out and deliver these nourishing packages to a local food bank.

The Inspiration

The idea of community is something that a child cannot learn too early. Celebrating the holidays by coming together to make breads and muffins, and then delivering them to those less fortunate is a special way to remind everyone what the spirit of the holidays is all about. This party focuses solely on baking with children, and we encourage you to include all of the guests in delivering their goods to food banks, or host a bake sale where the proceeds go to charity.

PROJECTS AND MATERIALS

Recipe card invitations
- decorative or vintage recipe card
- fine-point pen

Upcycled sweater aprons
- old wool sweaters
- sewing shears
- straight pins
- needle and thread
- double-fold bias tape
- ruler or yardstick

Inside decor
- wooden cutting boards and cheese boards
- linen tablecloths and napkins and silverware
- baskets to hold napkins and silverware
- bread baskets
- wooden crates
- pine greens and vases
- beeswax candles

Wrapping station
- paper bags
- colored cellophane or tissue paper
- scissors
- tape
- ribbons

Watercolor blessings
- watercolor paper and paints and brushes
- recycled glass jars for water

Recipes
- Baked Brie with Sautéed Pears
- Carrot-Apple Muffins with Crystallized Ginger
- Chocolate-Orange Bread

TIMELINE

2 weeks to 1 month prior to event:
- contact your local food bank to see if they have any restrictions on home-baked goods
- create and deliver invitations

1 week prior to event:
- gather all table decor and dishware
- go thrifting for wool sweaters (to be made into aprons)
- make upcycled sweater aprons

Day prior to event:
- gather all recipe ingredients
- clean all equipment and inventory necessary pans
- gather brown paper bags and cut them into large sheets to use as wrapping paper
- gather other wrapping and labeling supplies
- make one batch of each bread recipe (only if you would like guests to sample finished breads they are making)

Day of event:
- organize each recipe by ingredients
- print copies of recipes (one per child)
- set up the cooking table, wrapping station, and watercolor painting area so that they are ready upon their arrival)

Create Invitations

• Write the details of your community cooking party on a decorative or vintage recipe card. You may choose to include a recipe for one of the baked goods at this time as a temptation.

• Hand-deliver invitations to each guest.

Make Upcycled Sweater Aprons

We recommend making these awesome aprons as the take-away gift from the party.

materials:

½ yard of fabric such as a felted sweater

I package double-fold bias tape (at least 3 yards)

needle and thread

instructions:

• To felt a wool sweater, find an old sweater (thrift stores will have a lot) that is at least 80 percent wool. Wash it with soap in hot water and dry on high heat. The sweater should shrink and tighten into a solid piece of fabric. Cut sleeves off at seams. Cut side seams. Save any buttons for embellishing.

• Enlarge pattern (on page 121 to size and cut out pattern template. Place where indicated on fold of fabric, pin, and cut. Because you are beginning with a felted sweater, the pattern template will not always fit exactly on the fabric at hand. That's okay — it just means you will have a completely unique apron! The beauty of this pattern is that it is versatile. All that matters is that you have the basic shape and it fits the child it is intended for. In fact, once you cut the sweater apart at the seams, you may find that you like the look of it more than the apron pattern provided. Go with it! The basic instructions remain the same whatever shape your apron takes on.

• Trim edges with bias tape or ribbon if you prefer a finished edge, or leave as is (felted wool will not unravel).

• Cut a length of bias tape 72 inches long. Find the center of the bias tape, measure 10 inches from each side of the center (leaving a 20-inch loop for neck), and pin to top corners of apron. Sandwich the apron armholes between the bias tape and pin to the end of the curved edge. Leave bias tape long for ties.

• Beginning at one long end of the bias tape, sew around all ties, armholes, and neck loop of apron.

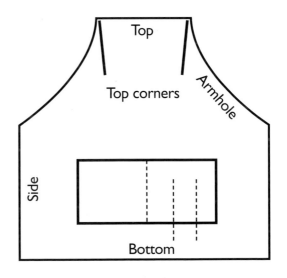

- To add pockets, cut a square or rectangle from the apron fabric or contrasting fabric. If using a felted sweater, the sleeve works perfectly for this. (I like my pockets to be approximately 8 inches wide × 5 inches tall.) The ribbed band of most sweaters looks nice as the top of the pocket. Pin the pocket in place and sew around the side and bottom edges. If you would like a divided pocket, sew as many seams up the pocket as you would like. (I like to make one in the center of the pocket and 2 or 3 to one side of the center, leaving one medium-size pocket and 3 or 4 small pockets for spoons, etc.)

- To embellish the apron further, sew buttons where the neck strap meets the apron, appliqué a design or embroider a name on the pocket before sewing it onto the apron, add rickrack or ribbon stripes across the bottom of the apron, or add a pocket to the chest of the apron.

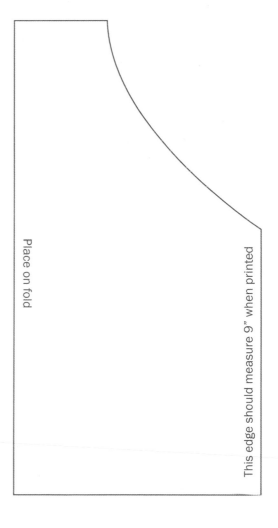

Place on fold

This edge should measure 9" when printed

Set the Scene

Since this party takes place mostly **in your kitchen**, use the baking ingredients as part of the setting for this party. Glass jars full of flour and sugar, large ceramic or glass bowls filled with fruits and vegetables that are included in the recipes, creamers containing liquid ingredients, and large containers of utensils act as lovely, practical centerpieces. You may also add pine greens and candles to decorate the table.

Hang the **sweater aprons** from a row of hooks or an interior clothesline. You can make them for individual attendees or allow the children to choose their favorites to take home from the party.

Make and bake some of the bread and muffins before your guests arrive. This will give the house a wonderful aroma, a sense of warmth and joy, as well as something for the guests to taste and enjoy. Seeing the table set with muffins and breads is a great way for kids to know what they are making.

Set up a small **tea bar** where the kids can smell different varieties of teas and sample a few of the flavors between baking batches.

Candles are always wonderful for any party, but they have a special place around the kitchen. Light a few **beeswax candles**, turn on some music, and get the kids into a very festive mood.

Create a **wrapping station** on wooden crates or a low table. Include sheets of brown paper (cut from recycled bags), colored cellophane or tissue paper, scissors, ribbons, and tape for the children to use when wrapping baked goods for delivery. For further embellishments of the packages, set out sheets of watercolored paper that kids can cut designs out of to add to the packages.

Create a **watercolor painting area** with an easel or tabletop space, watercolor paints, jars of water, paintbrushes, paper, and colored pencils. Allow children to watercolor paper and then either write a blessing or draw a picture to include as a nice topping to the packages. (It takes only about 7 minutes for watercolors to dry.)

Food Fun and Recipes

The process of cooking for others, specially wrapping the gifts, and then hand-delivering them is more than a party — it's a celebration of community. If time allows, plan a trip to the food bank or shelter to deliver your freshly baked goods. If you cannot work this out at the close of the party, plan a separate time when you can all gather again (soon after the party) to make deliveries.

BAKED BRIE WITH SAUTÉED PEARS

This recipe is intended to keep tummies happy while the baking for community happens. Prepare it in advance of or at the very beginning of the party for your guests to enjoy.

- ½ cup slivered almonds
- 1 small wheel of brie
- 4 tablespoons (½ stick) butter
- 2 pears, in ½-inch slices
- 1 tablespoon brown sugar

Preheat oven to 325°F. Place almonds in a single layer on a baking sheet and roast for 5 minutes. Remove from oven and set aside to cool. Increase oven temperature to 350°F.

Place the wooden container (any plastic removed) of brie in a larger baking dish and bake until melted and bubbly, about 7 minutes.

While the brie is baking, melt butter in a large skillet, then add the pears and sugar. Sauté until golden brown, and set aside.

Assemble the baked brie, pears, and almonds on a platter, and serve with crackers or flatbread.

Serves 6

Carrot-Apple Muffins with Crystallized Ginger

We recommend making 3 batches of these muffins to deliver.

2 cups all-purpose flour

1 teaspoon baking soda

¼ teaspoon baking powder

1 teaspoon ground cinnamon

1 teaspoon ground ginger

¼ teaspoon salt

½ cup honey

⅓ cup vegetable oil

2 large eggs

1 teaspoon vanilla extract

⅓ cup milk

1 cup shredded carrots

1 cup shredded apple

2 tablespoons minced crystallized ginger

Preheat oven to 350°F. Line or grease muffin pans.

In a large bowl, sift together flour, baking soda, baking powder, cinnamon, ginger, and salt. Set aside.

In the bowl of an electric mixer fitted with the paddle attachment, combine the honey, oil, eggs, and vanilla. Add the dry ingredients to the wet and mix just to combine.

Add the milk to moisten if needed, one tablespoon at a time. Fold in the carrots, apple, and crystallized ginger. Fill each muffin cup three-quarters full and bake for 18–22 minutes, or until a toothpick inserted in the center of a muffin comes out clean. Remove from oven and allow to cool in the muffin tins before removing.

Makes 18 muffins

CHOCOLATE-ORANGE BREAD

We recommend making 4 batches of this bread to deliver.

1½ cups all-purpose flour

½ cup unsweetened cocoa powder

½ teaspoon salt

½ teaspoon baking powder

½ teaspoon baking soda

8 tablespoons (1 stick) butter, softened

1 cup granulated sugar

2 large eggs

1 teaspoon vanilla extract

zest of 1 orange

1 cup buttermilk

¼ cup minced candied orange peel

¼ cup semisweet chocolate chips

Preheat oven to 350°F. Lightly spray a 9 x 5-inch loaf pan with oil and set aside.

Sift the flour, cocoa powder, salt, baking powder, and baking soda together in a large bowl and set aside.

In the bowl of an electric mixer, cream the butter and sugar together until fluffy. Add the eggs, one at a time. Add the vanilla and orange zest.

With the mixer on low speed, alternate between adding the buttermilk and the dry ingredients, mixing just to combine. When well mixed, fold in the candied orange peel and chocolate chips.

Bake for 55–60 minutes, or until a toothpick comes out clean. Cool for about 15 minutes, then carefully turn out and finish cooling on a cooling rack.

Makes 1 loaf

TABLE OF EQUIVALENTS

Some of the conversions in these lists have been slightly rounded for measuring convenience.

VOLUME

U.S.	metric
¼ teaspoon	1.25 milliliters
½ teaspoon	2.5 milliliters
¾ teaspoon	3.75 milliliters
1 teaspoon	5 milliliters
1 tablespoon (3 teaspoons)	15 milliliters
2 tablespoons	30 milliliters
3 tablespoons	45 milliliters
1 fluid ounce (2 tablespoons)	30 milliliters
¼ cup (4 tablespoons)	60 milliliters
⅓ cup	80 milliliters
½ cup	120 milliliters
⅔ cup	160 milliliters
1 cup	240 milliliters
2 cups (1 pint)	480 milliliters
4 cups (1 quart or 32 ounces)	960 milliliters
1 gallon (4 quarts)	3.8 liters

WEIGHT:

U.S.	metric
1 ounce (by weight)	28 grams
1 pound	448 grams
2.2 pounds	1 kilogram

LENGTH:

U.S.	metric
⅛ inch	3 millimeters
¼ inch	6 millimeters
½ inch	12 millimeters
1 inch	2.5 centimeters

OVEN TEMPERATURE:

Fahrenheit	Celsius
250	120
275	140
300	150
325	160
350	180
375	190
400	200
425	220
450	230
475	240
500	260

Resources

ANNI'S WEBSITES

Bamboo~conscious family living magazine
www.bamboofamilymag.com

Organically Raised Cookbook
www.organicallyraisedcookbook.com

Ice Pop Joy
www.icepopjoy.com

Sacred Pregnancy
www.sacredpregnancy.com

Food and Life Styling / Delicious Gratitude
www.deliciousgratitude.com

HEATHER'S WEBSITES

Shivaya Naturals Blog
www.shivayanaturals.com

Rhythm of the Home Magazine
www.rhythmofthehome.com

PHOTOGRAPHERS

Tnah Louise + Mario Di Donato (primary photographers)
www.bellafacciafoto.com

Rebecca Coyle (contributor)
www.rebeccacoyle.com

Heather Fontenot (contributor)
www.shivayanaturals.com

Alexandra DeFurio (contributor)
www.defuriophotography.com

Ginney Sheller (contributor)
Small Things (www.gsheller.com)

Elwood Spedden (contributor)

Anni's Acknowledgments

My family, especially my husband Tim, who is always my greatest champion and dearest friend, are the support that makes everything possible. Thank you my love.

To my children, Zoe, Lotus, Bodhi, and River, Mommy loves you dearly! I am looking forward to celebrating many passing seasons with all of you for many years to come.

To my mom for her endless love and support, I love you. And to my in-laws, Bonnie and Dan, for your generous support and care.

Tnah and Mario, thank you for stepping up and helping me create this book! Your pictures are beautiful and it was so much fun hanging out with you guys, looking through pictures, and catching all the great angles of each and every party.

Rebecca, you saved my life by stepping in at the last moment, and I deeply appreciate that. Your photography is gorgeous and you are becoming a good friend. I adore you and your cuties, Riley and Rowan!

Thank you, Heather, for hanging in there and being my writing partner. You are an amazing woman, and I am honored to have shared this experience with you.

Thank you, Rose, for the use of your gorgeous collection of goodies and your rose garden. Thank you, Milla, for playing dress-up with us, and Wes, for lugging stuff with Tim and hanging out all day and night at the beach party shoot!

Thank you to my amazing editor, Megan Hiller, at Sellers. I know this was down to the wire, but I am so grateful for your willingness to hang in there and work with me to get this book finished!

Thank you to all the gorgeous children who lent their smiles and good cheer to each of these parties!

Thank you, Ginney Sheller, for helping with the egg-dyeing party. You are an amazing mother and blogger, and your children are very lucky!

Thank you to Juney Bloom (juneybloomclothing.com) for the gorgeous dresses for use at the faerie party. Susan, you are an incredible designer, and I am grateful.

I thank you to Michele Brule from Enchanted Enfant (enchantedenfant.com) for your gorgeous dresses! They are precious.

Thank you to David Ellison from the Lorimer Workshop, John Duffy from Stable Tables, and Michael "Bug" Deakin from Heritage Salvage for your amazing farm tables to help prop up these gorgeous pictures. (www.heritagesalvage.com; www.tablesbenches.com; www.lorimerantiques.myshopify.com)

Erin Wallace (tinytwistcreative.com), you are amazing. Your willingness to jump in and help me so quickly is astounding. I am grateful.

Candy Ailstock, thank you for working so quickly to help me out and for your complete willingness to help me get those aprons done!

Thank you to Sarah at Sarah Silks for giving us those gorgeous silk wings to share at the faerie party. (http://sarahssilks.com)

Thank you to Rebecca Varon Felting (www.nushkie.etsy.com) for the awesome wands! You are an amazing felter.

Christy and Juan, thank you for the use of your gorgeous retro camper for the pancake party. You are dear friends and I honor the work you do in the world. Belly Sprout is luck to have you! (www.bellysprout.com)

Thank you to Luann and Rachel for your friendship and support.

Thank you to Elizabeth Shabazi for your knitted cozies and prop usage!

Thank you to Susan and Juliet for the use of your house and props for the book. You are both so lovely.

Thank you to Mark Kelly at Lodge Cast Iron for the use of your amazing products and GreenPots (my fave cook-ware). (www.lodgemfg.com; www.greencookingpots.com/)

Thank you to Rheiana for your scrumptious healthy donuts and for the recipes. Your donuts are heavenly! Check her out! (www.greencookingpots.com/)

Thank you to the Essential Oil Company for your beautifully smelling oils that "made" the spa day! Yummy… (www.essentialoil.com)

Thank you to Tara from Wrecked for the beautiful chalkboard that enhanced winter girl's honoring party and to Bearpawsticks — your talking sticks are amazing! (www.etsy.com/people/Wreckd; www.etsy.com/people/bear-pawsticks)

Thanks, Nova Natural Toys, for your support and willingness to always help me out. (www.novanatural.com)

Thank you Studio-Jones, Paper Source and Night Owl Paper Goods. (www.nightowlpapergoods.com; www.studio-jones.com; www.paper-source.com)

Thank you, Roxy Heart Vintage, for those awesome cake stands. (http://roxyheartvintage.com)

Thank you, Monica, at Eco Party Time. Your shop rocks! (www.ecopartytime.com)

Thank you, Bambeco folks! Your support is very important to me. (www.bambeco.com)

Thank you, Acme party folks, for your help and inspiration. Love the Crowns! (www.acmepartybox.com)

Thank you, Bake-it-pretty. Your shop is sweet and fun (www.bakeitpretty.com)

Heather's Acknowledgments

First, to Anni, for including me in this adventure. Thank you for your friendship and for sticking with me through it all. You are an amazing woman.

To my husband Joel, who has encouraged me to chase my dreams and has helped make so many come true already. Thank you for your support throughout these months and your willingness to taste-test oh so many recipes.

To my mother Phyllis, who is always there to hold a child, lend a hand, run to the store for a bunch of asparagus, and never lets me give up. Mom, you are the most amazing woman I know, and my best friend always.

To my children: Jacob, Elwood, and Landon. Thank you for choosing me to be your mama, and for the intense joy you bring to my life. You are my inspiration, in everything, and I love you more than you will ever know.

To Bernadette, for giving me the space to write this book while keeping Rhythm of the Home going. What would I do without you as my sounding board?

To Julia, for keeping me sane through your humor and friendship.

To all of the children who spent countless hours in front of the lens, thank you for your smiles, your joy, and for reminding me just what this book was all about.

Finally, to my father Elwood, whose strength and courage are awe-inspiring. Dad, I love you more than words could ever say. Thank you for the blessings you have brought to my life.